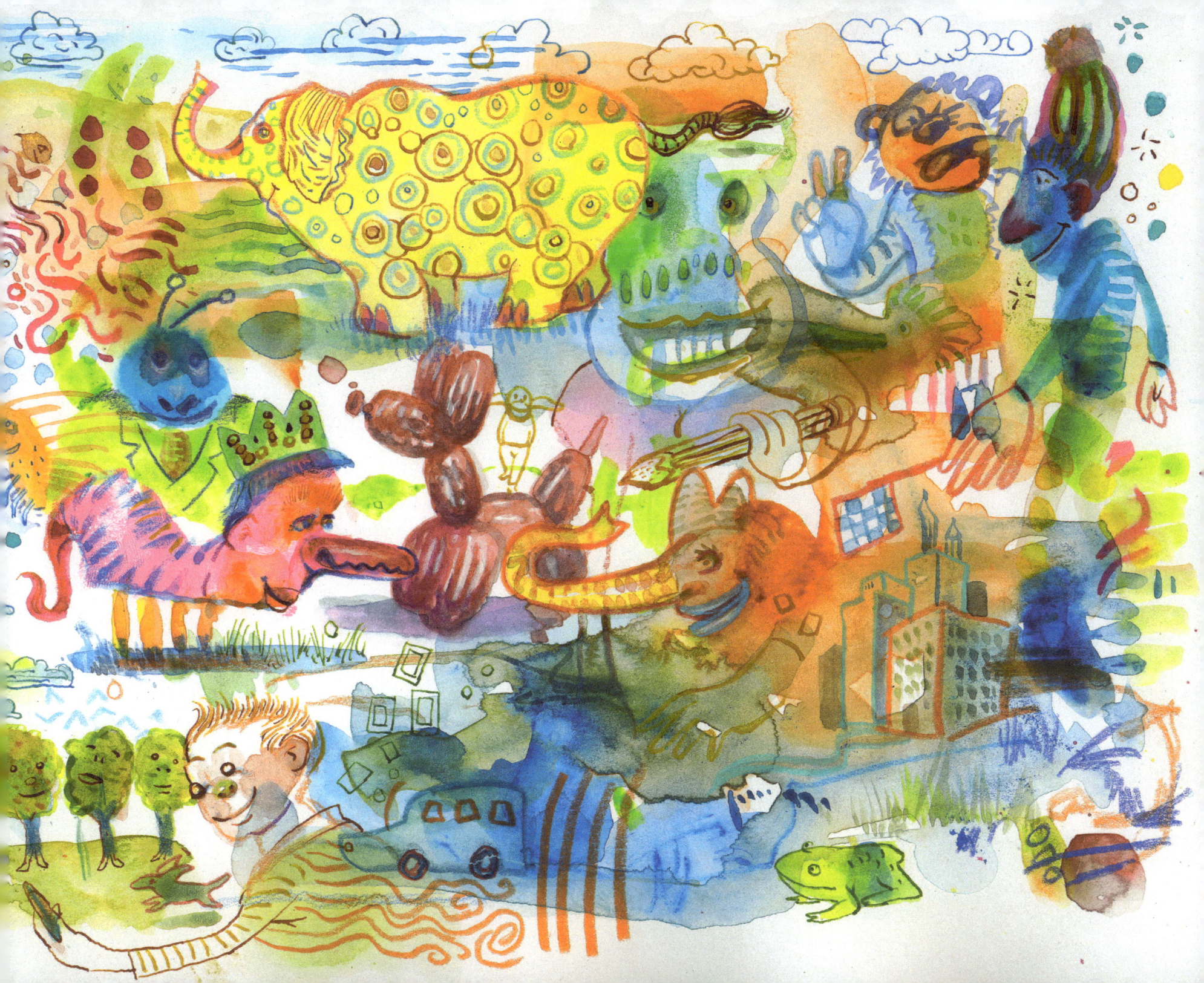

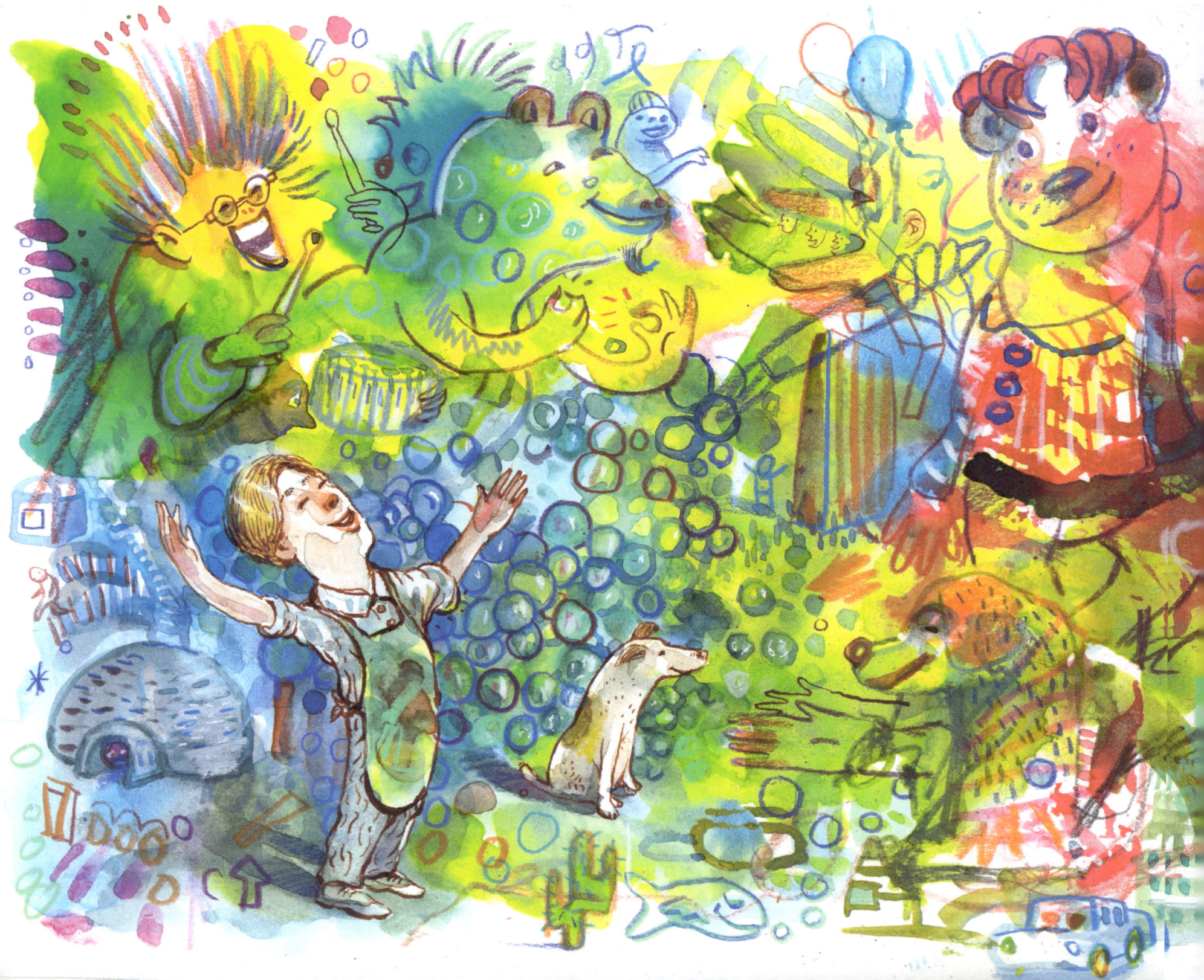

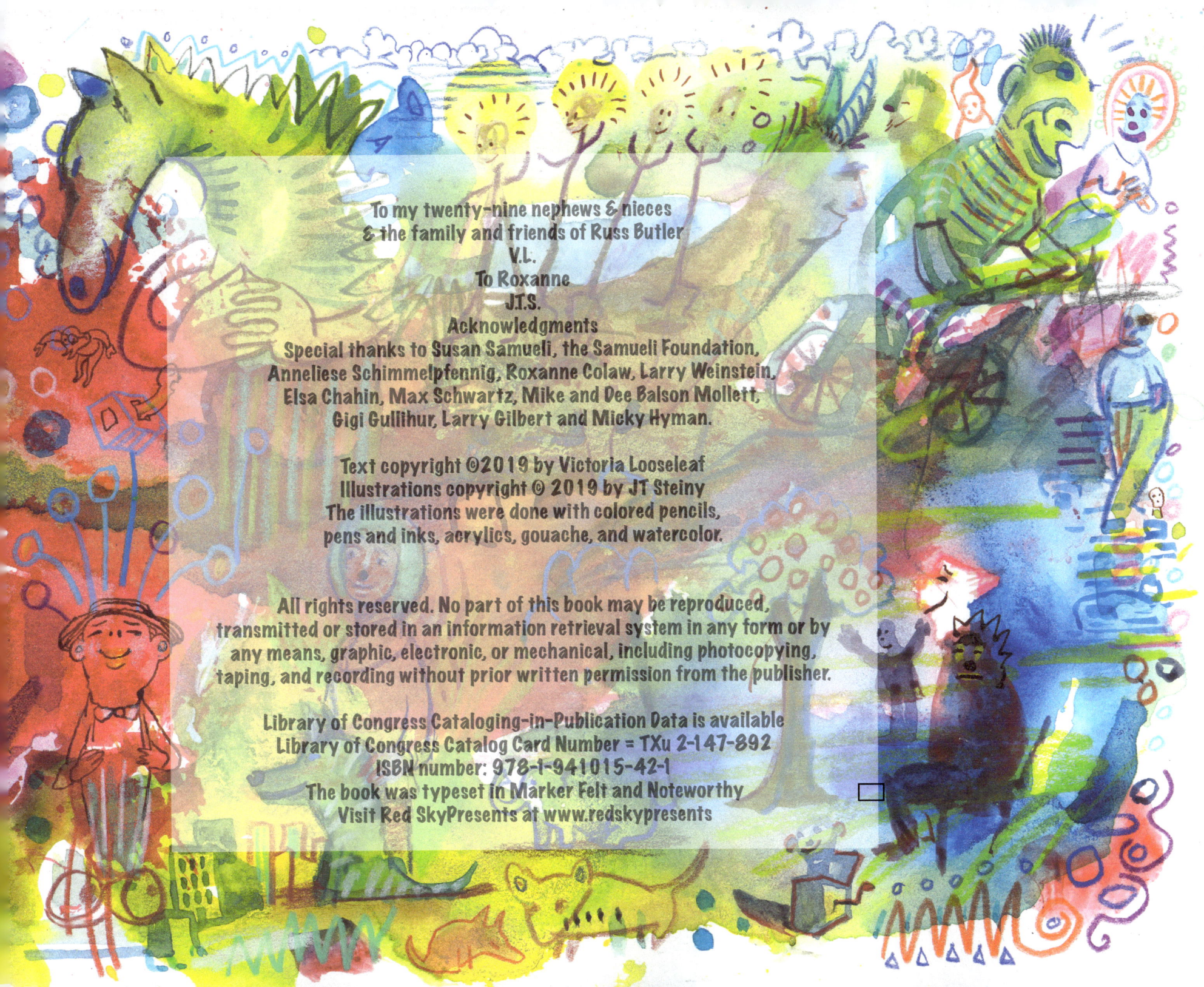

To my twenty-nine nephews & nieces
& the family and friends of Russ Butler
V.L.
To Roxanne
JT.S.
Acknowledgments
Special thanks to Susan Samueli, the Samueli Foundation,
Anneliese Schimmelpfennig, Roxanne Colaw, Larry Weinstein,
Elsa Chahin, Max Schwartz, Mike and Dee Balson Mollett,
Gigi Gullihur, Larry Gilbert and Micky Hyman.

Library of Congress Cataloging-in-Publication Data is available
Library of Congress Catalog Card Number = TXu 2-147-892
ISBN number: 978-1-941015-42-1
The book was typeset in Marker Felt and Noteworthy
Visit Red SkyPresents at www.redskypresents

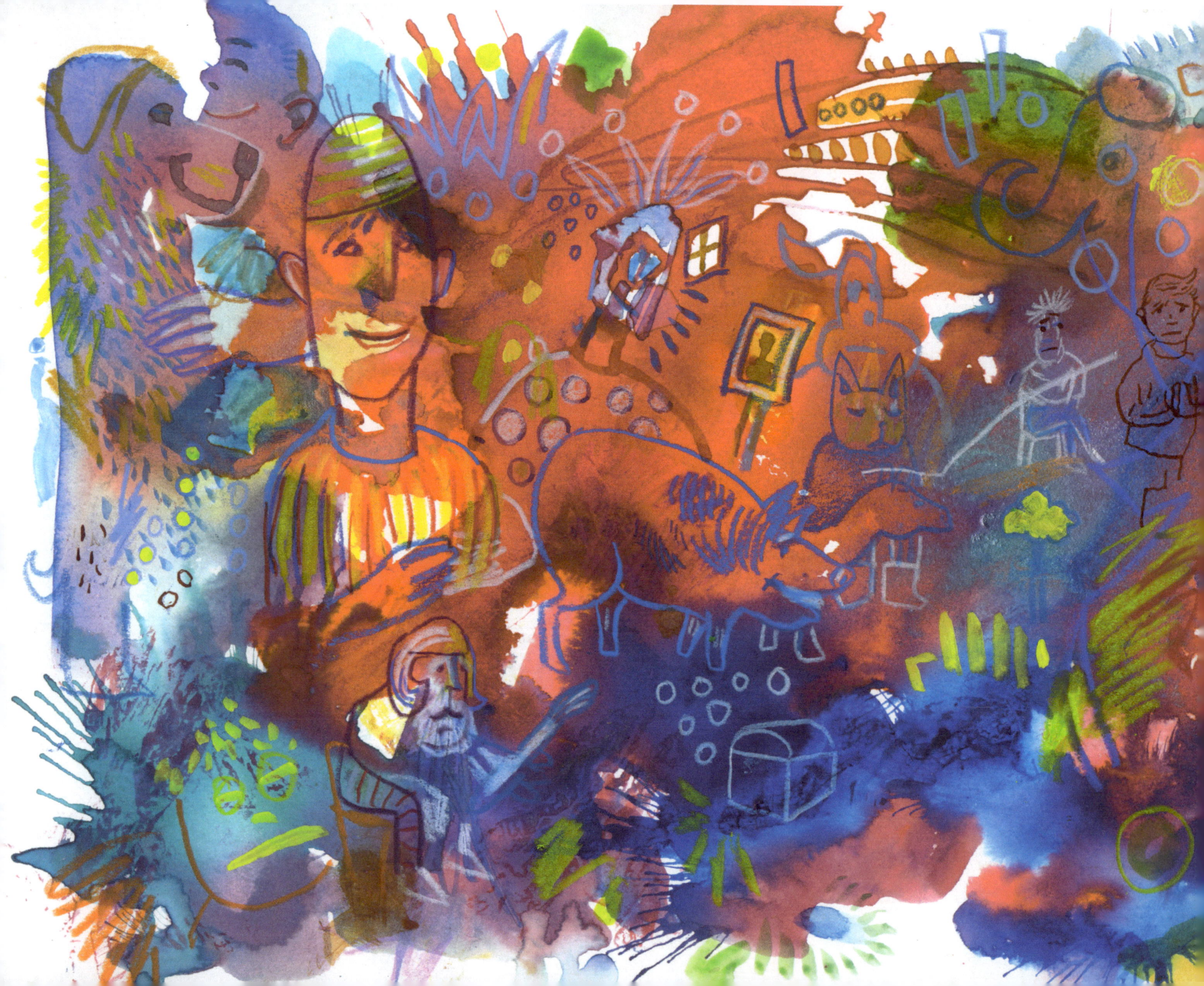

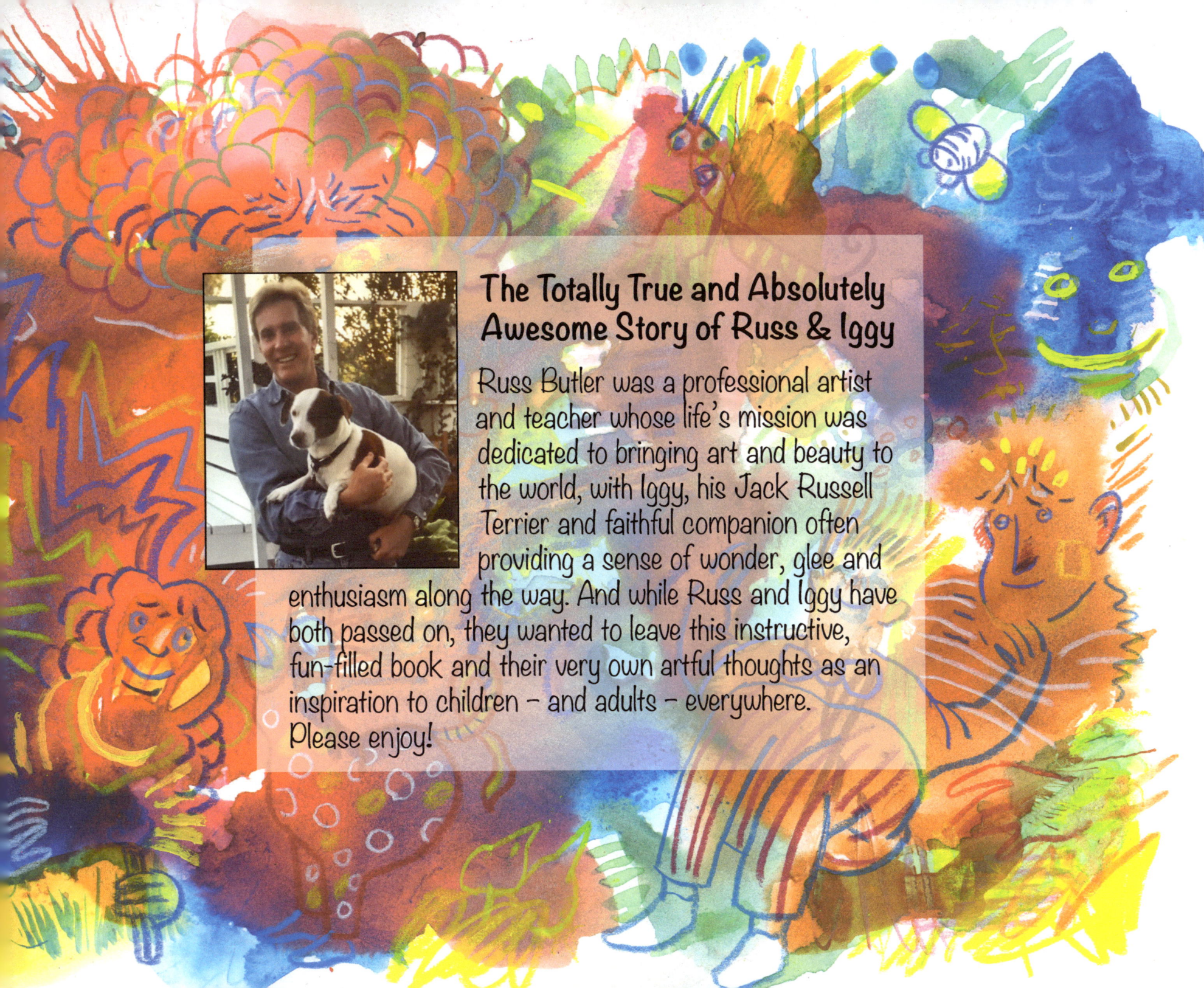

The Totally True and Absolutely Awesome Story of Russ & Iggy

Russ Butler was a professional artist and teacher whose life's mission was dedicated to bringing art and beauty to the world, with Iggy, his Jack Russell Terrier and faithful companion often providing a sense of wonder, glee and enthusiasm along the way. And while Russ and Iggy have both passed on, they wanted to leave this instructive, fun-filled book and their very own artful thoughts as an inspiration to children – and adults – everywhere. Please enjoy!

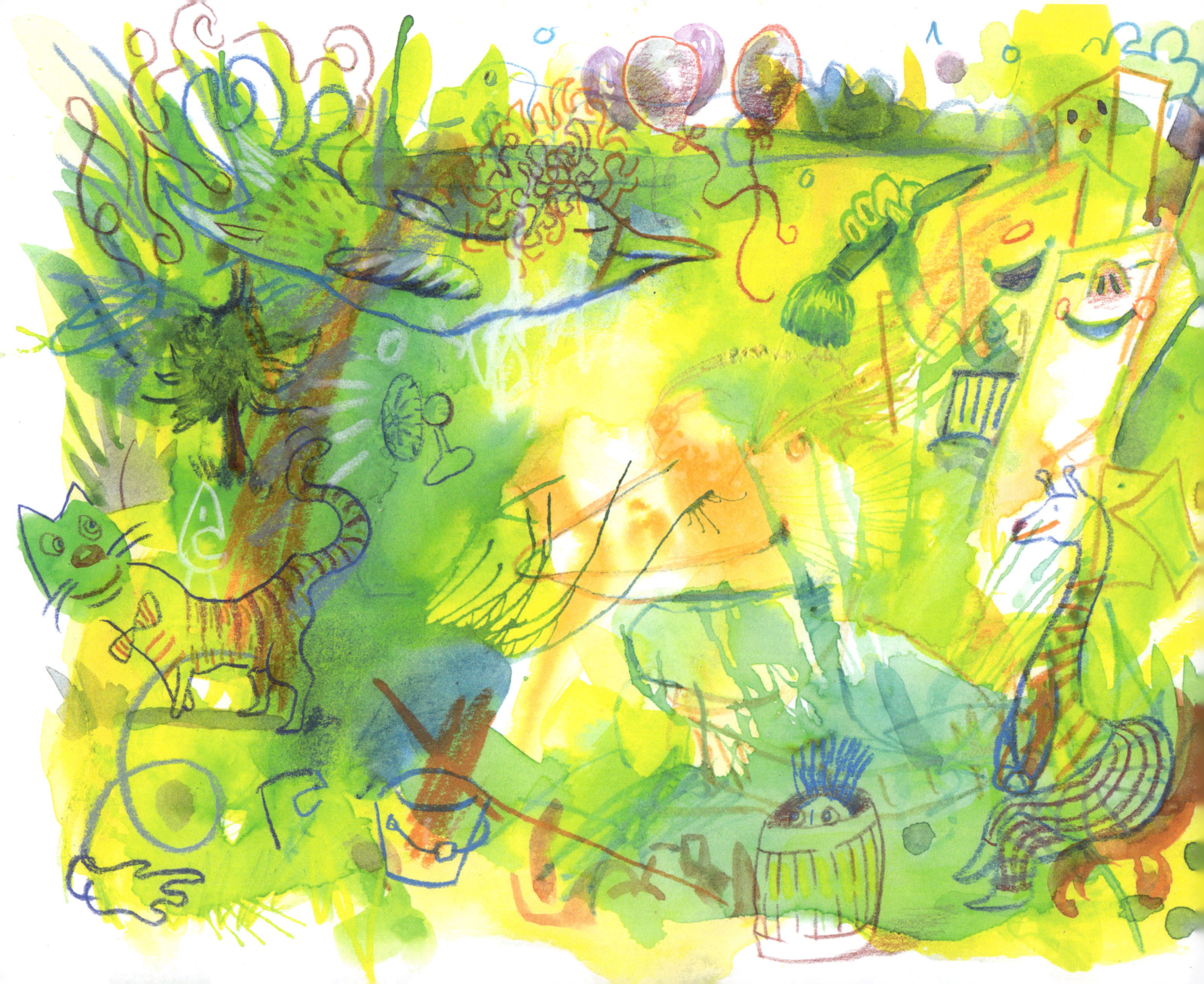

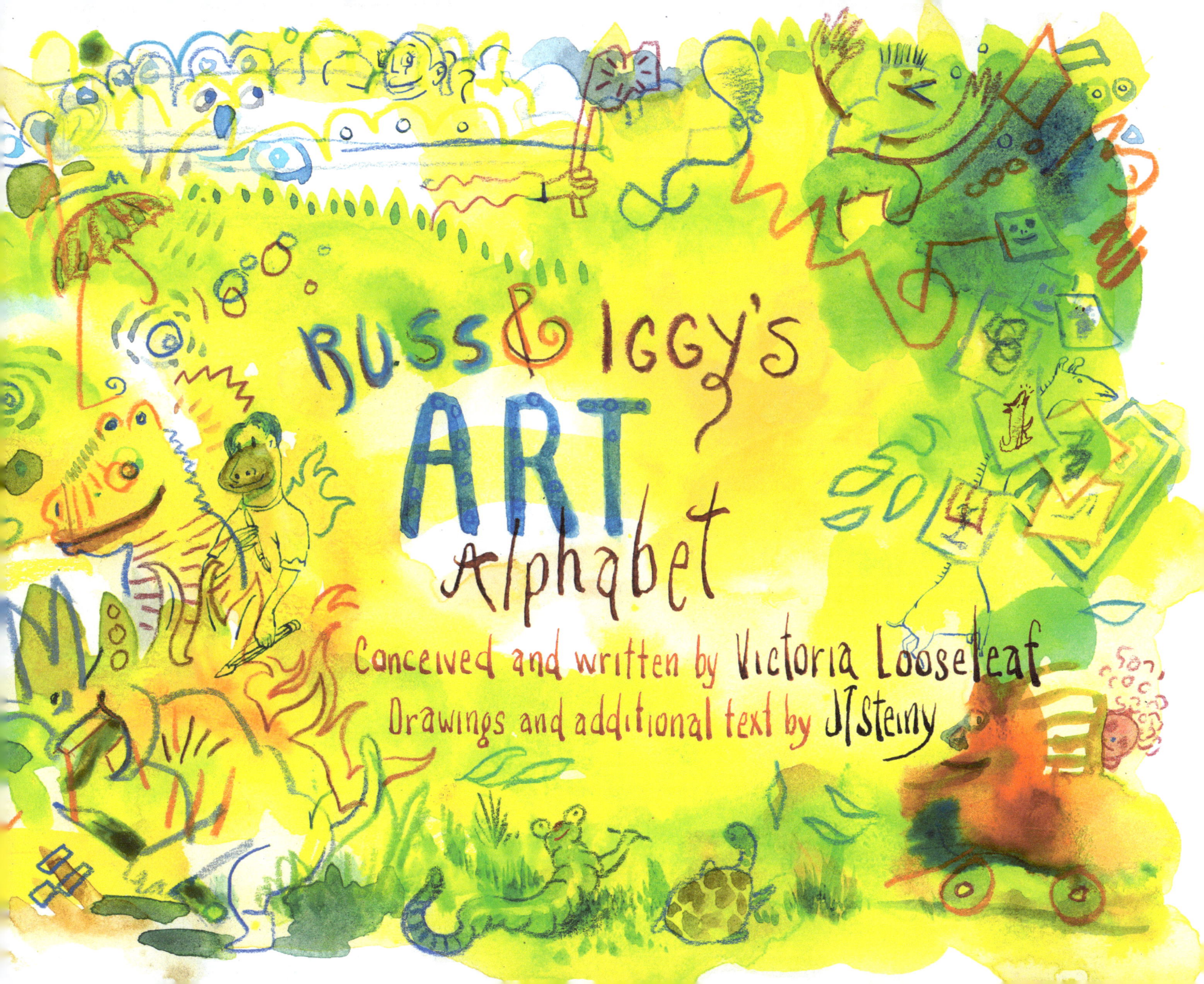

Russ & Iggy's ART Alphabet

Conceived and written by Victoria Looseleaf
Drawings and additional text by J Steiny

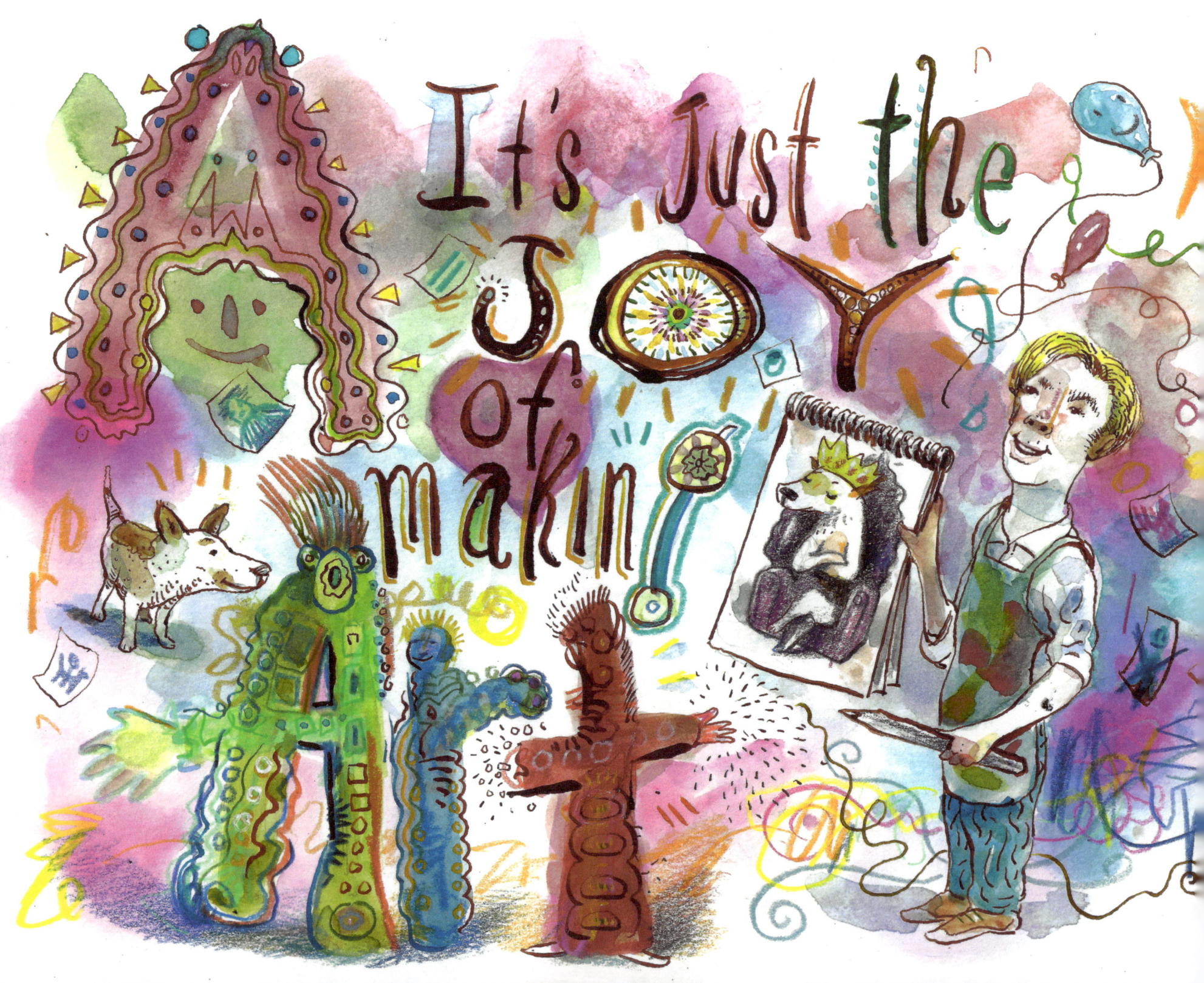

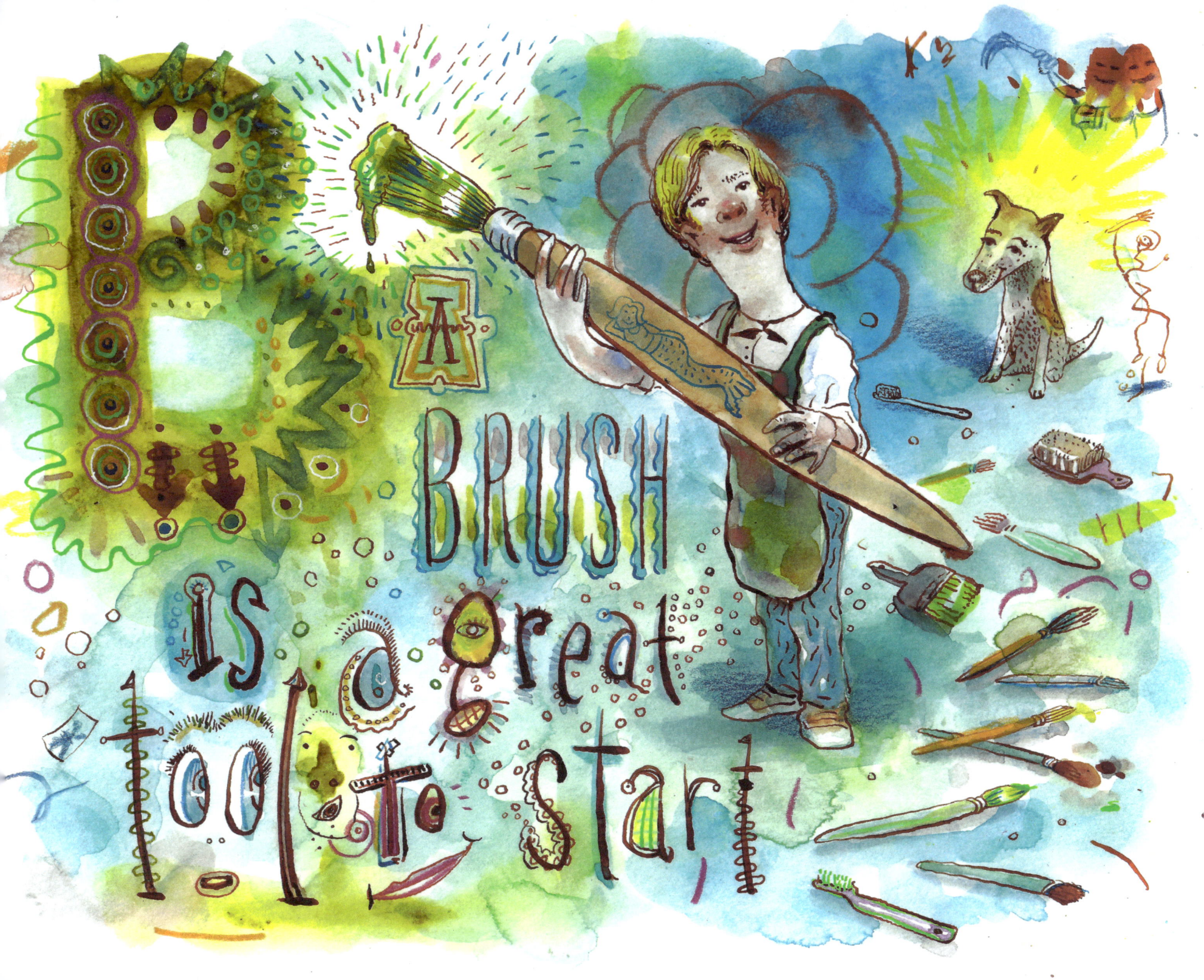

B is a great tool to start

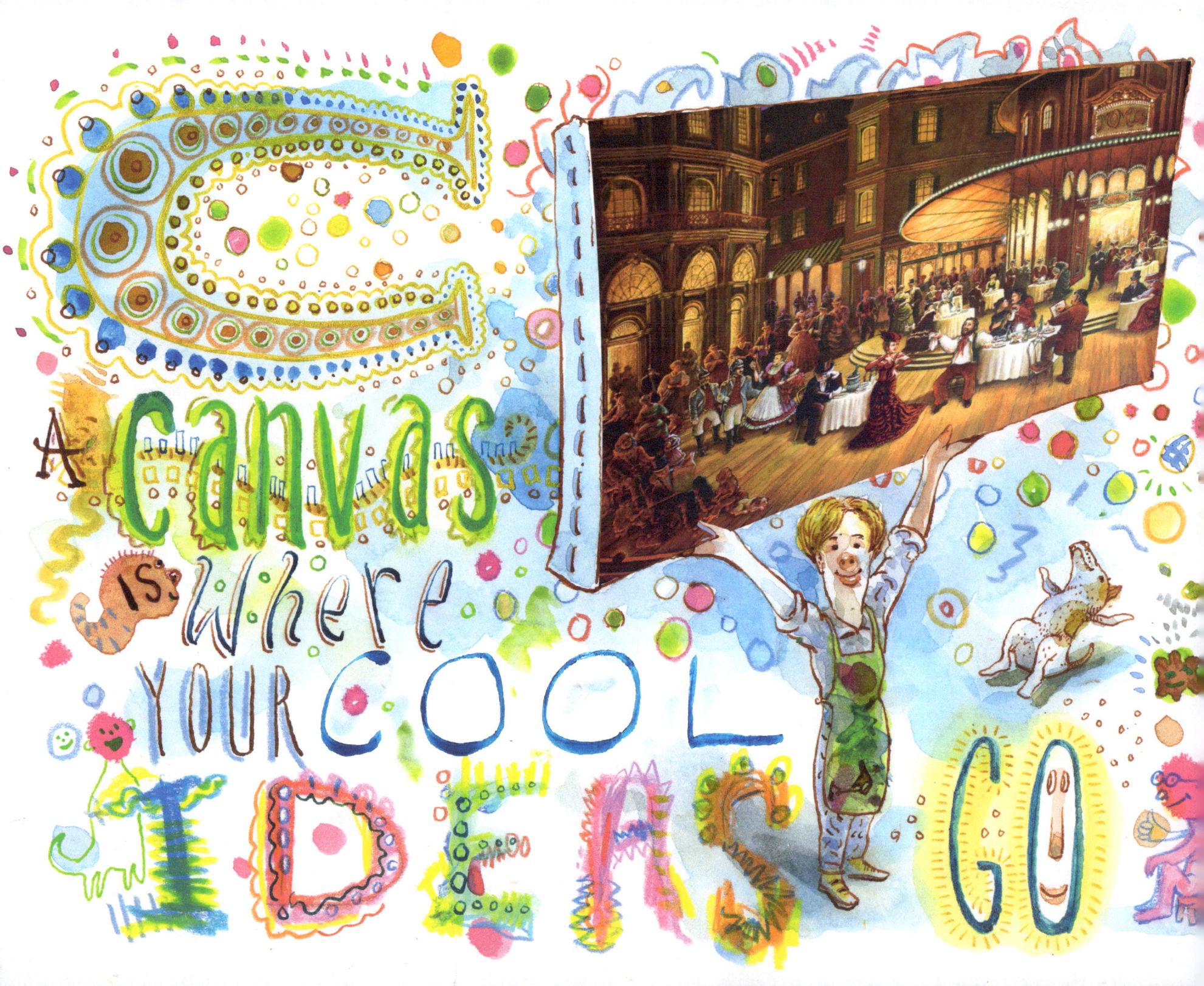

A canvas is where your COOL IDEAS GO

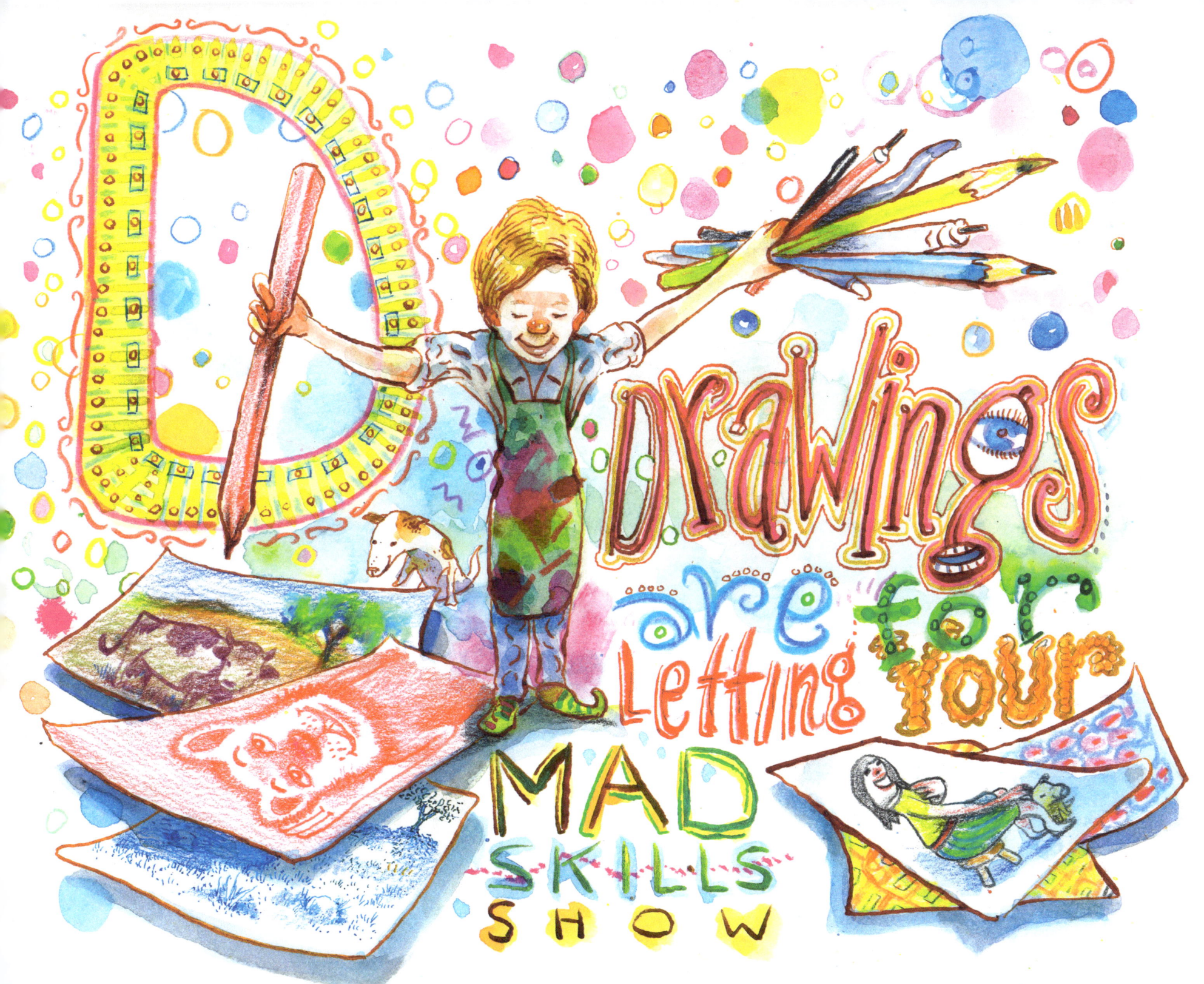

Drawings are for Letting your MAD SKILLS SHOW

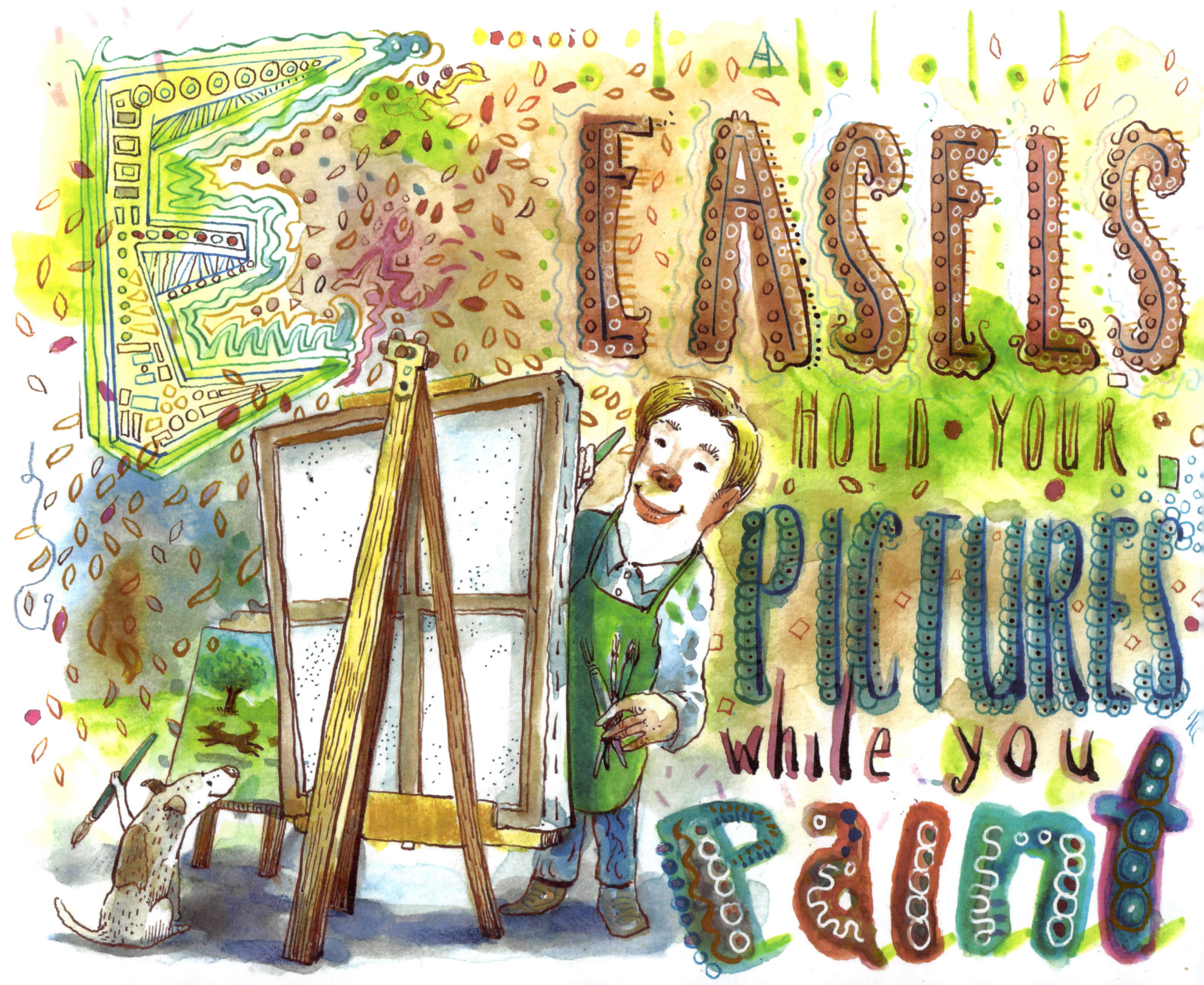

EASELS HOLD YOUR PICTURES while you paint

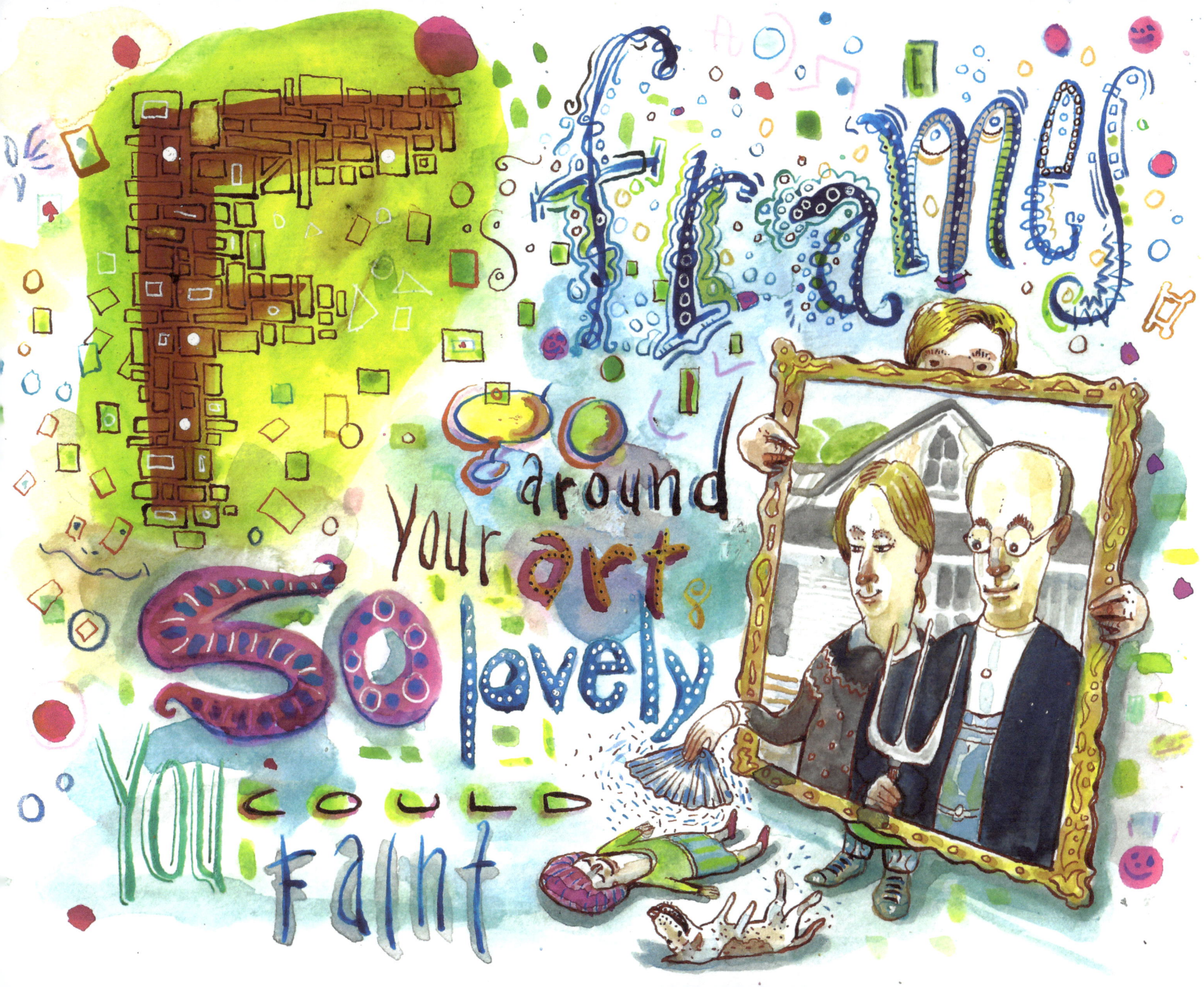

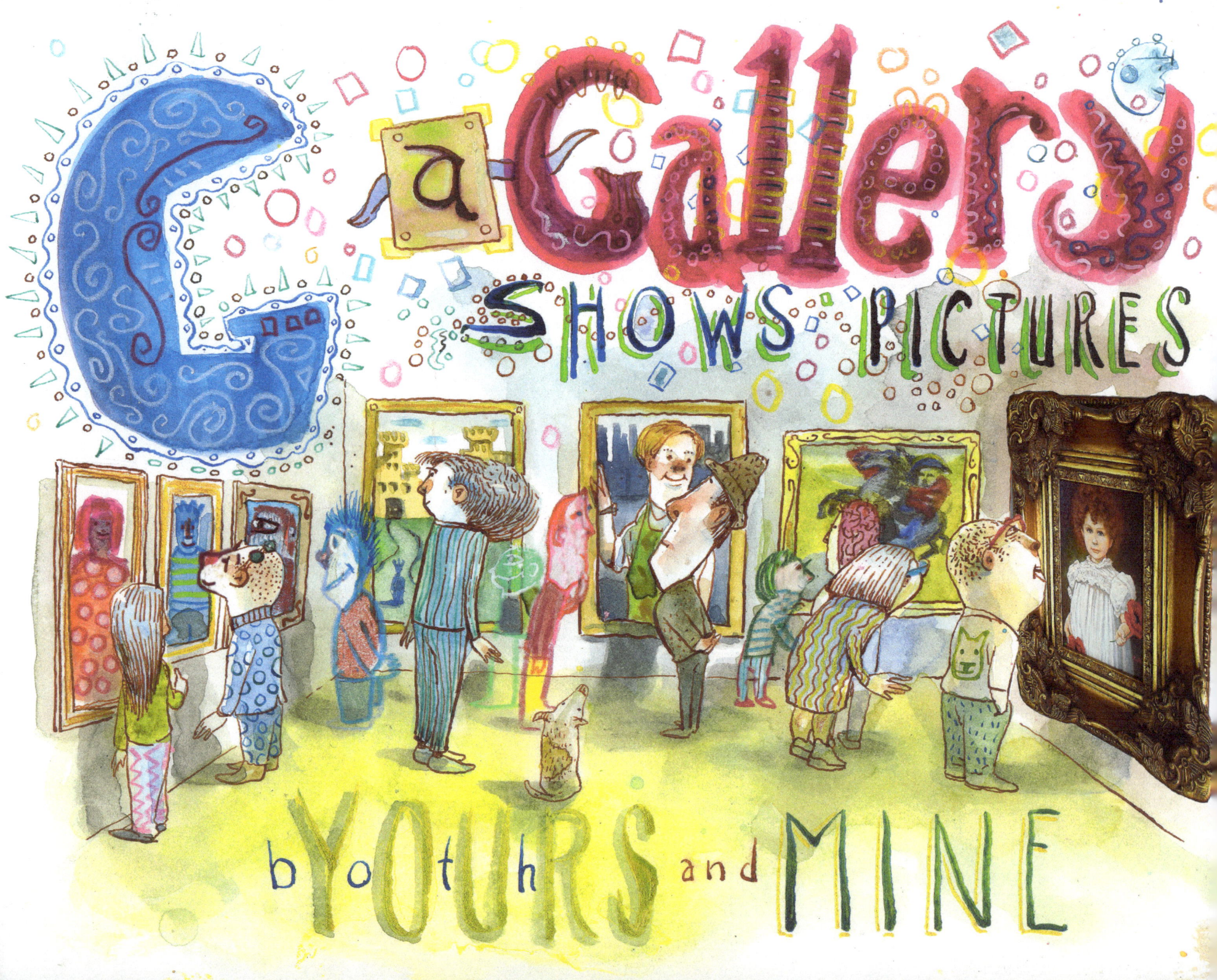

a Gallery shows pictures by YOURS (bYOotuhrs) and MINE

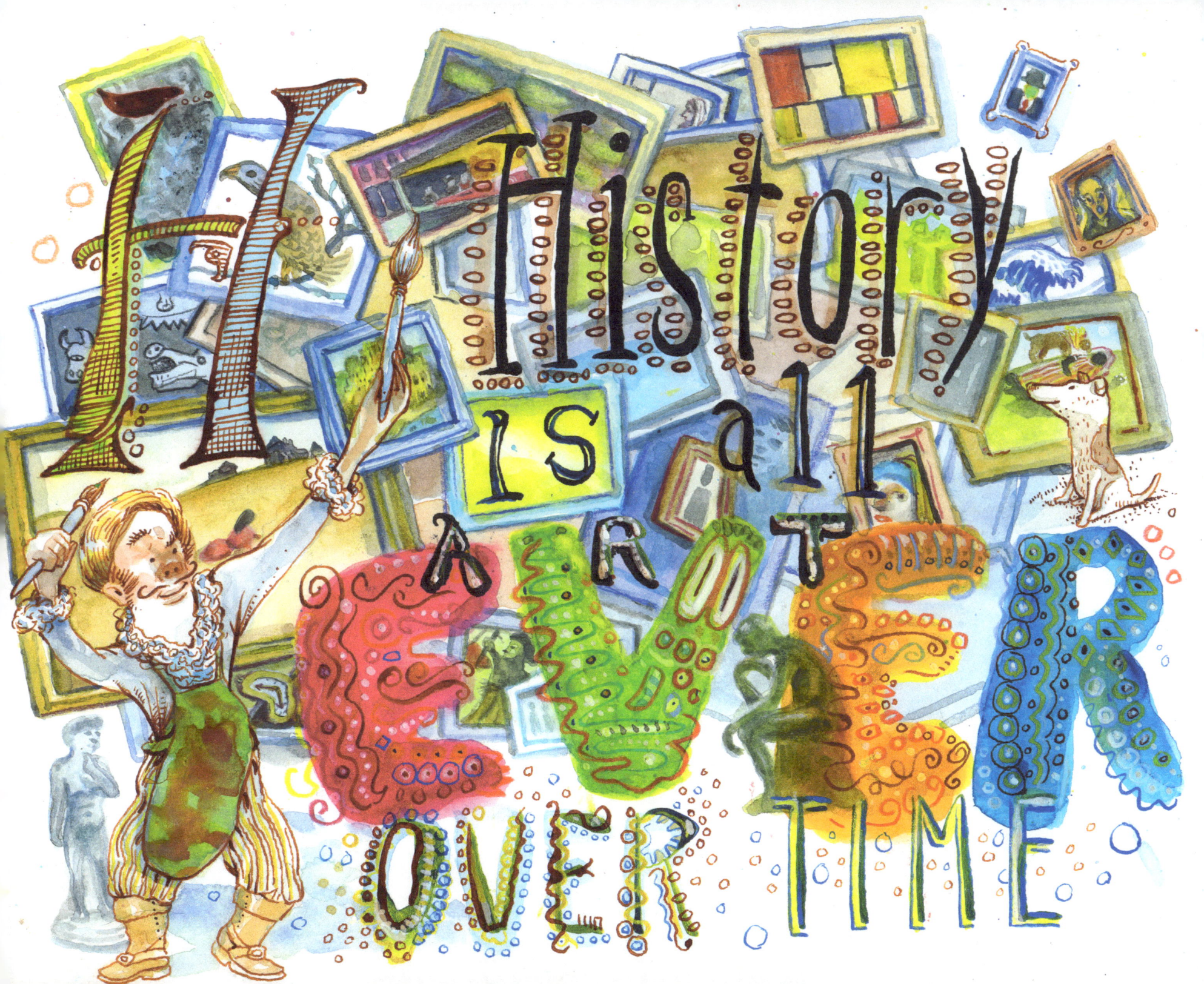

History is all ART over time

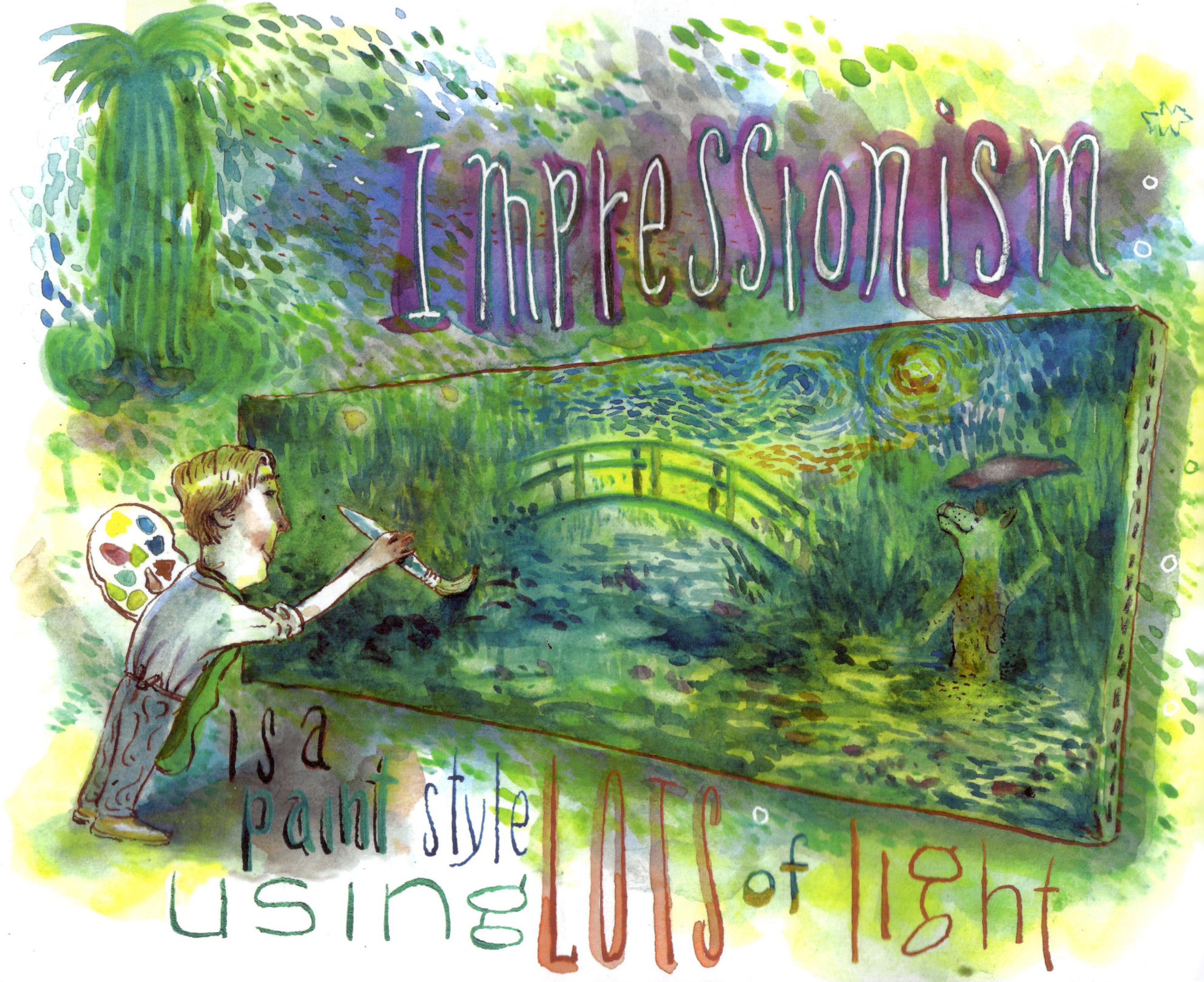

Impressionism

is a paint style using LOTS of light

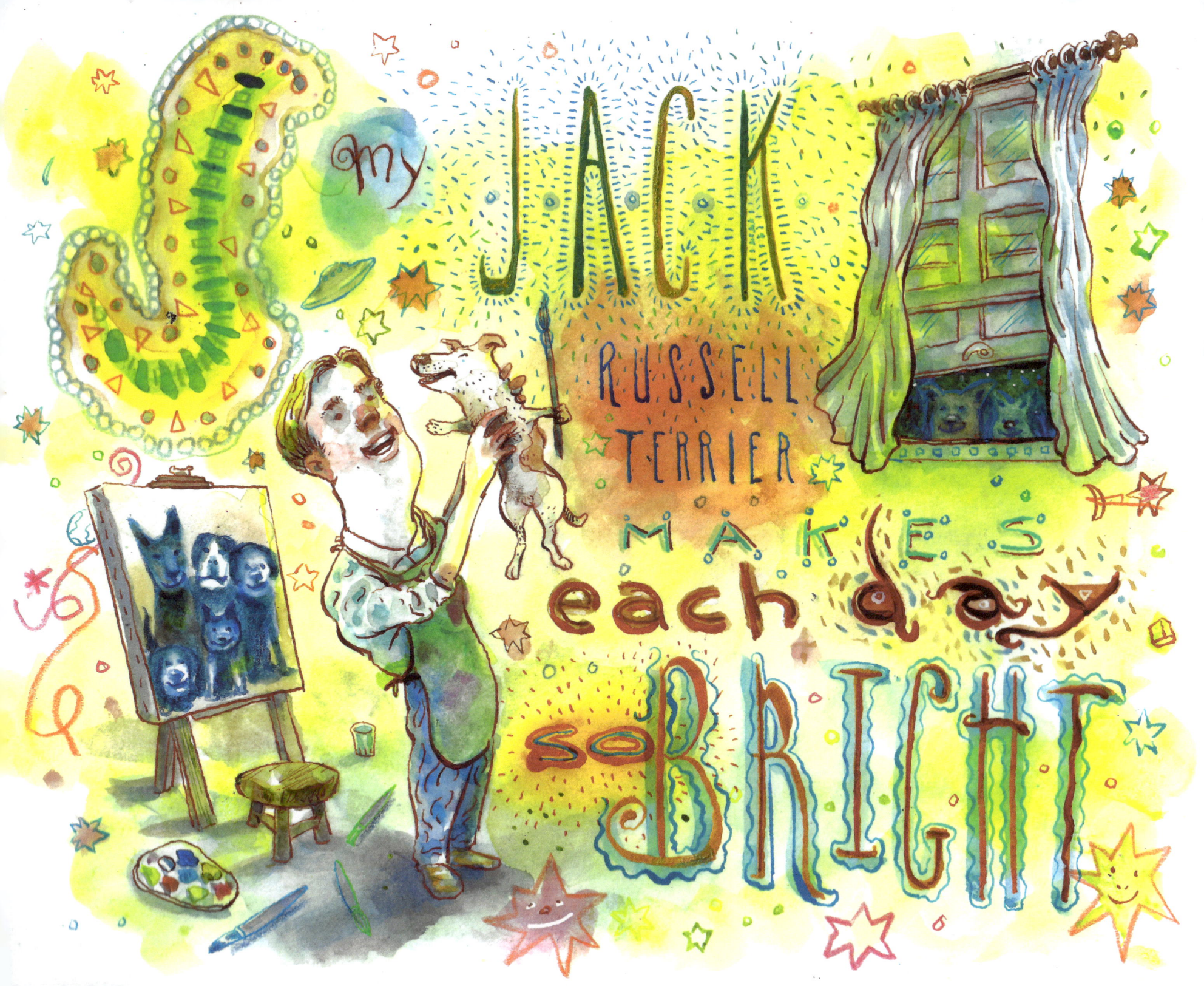

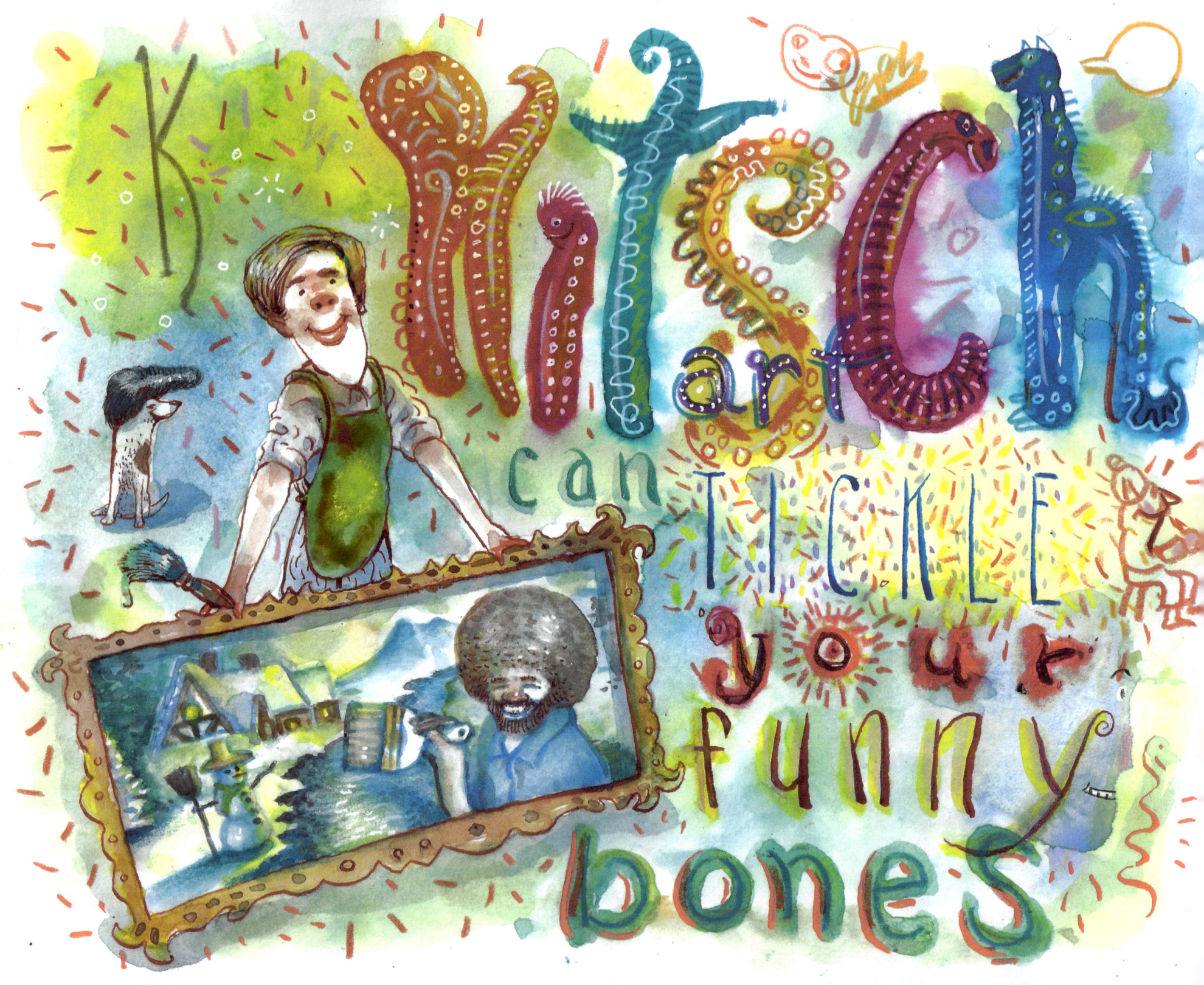

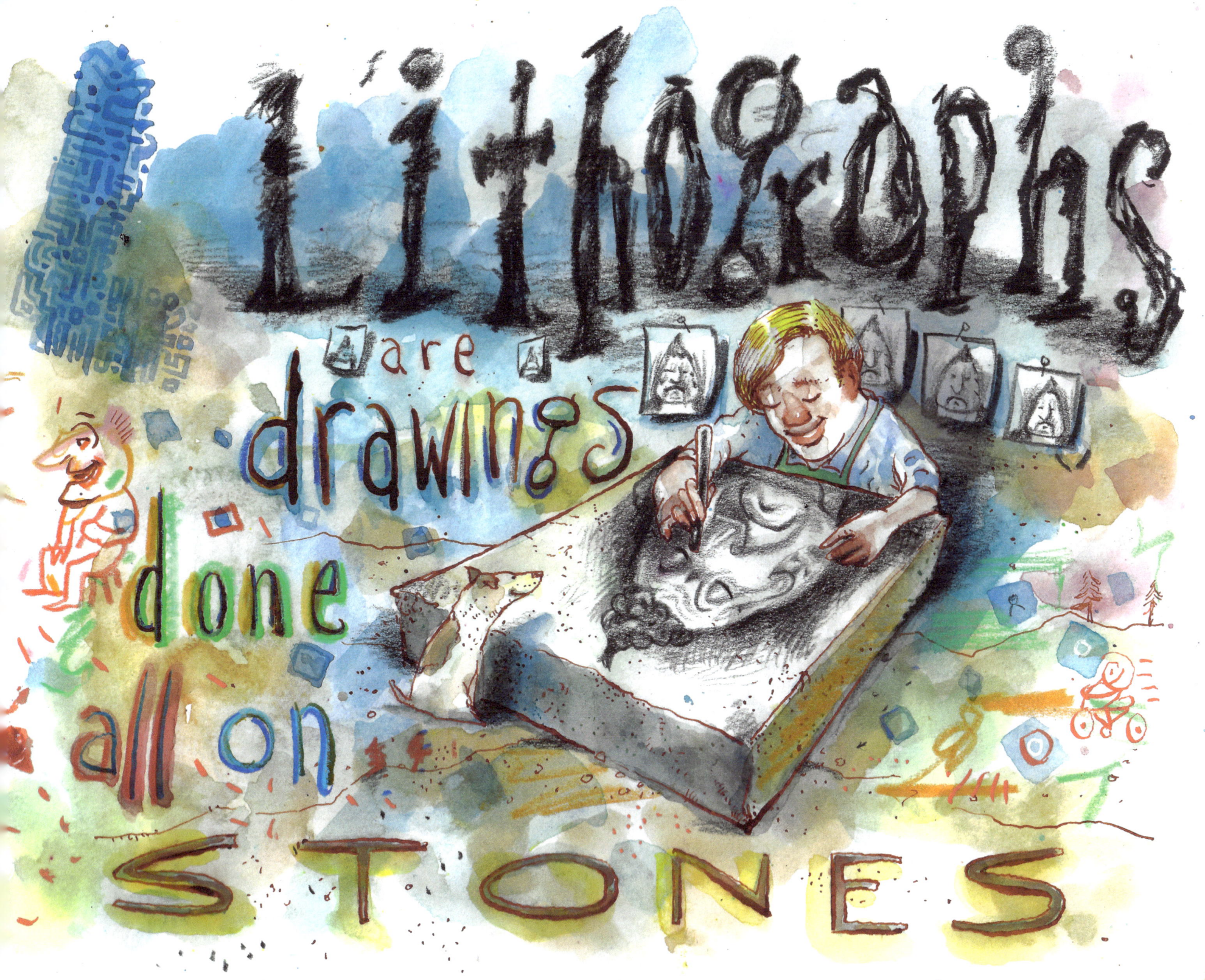

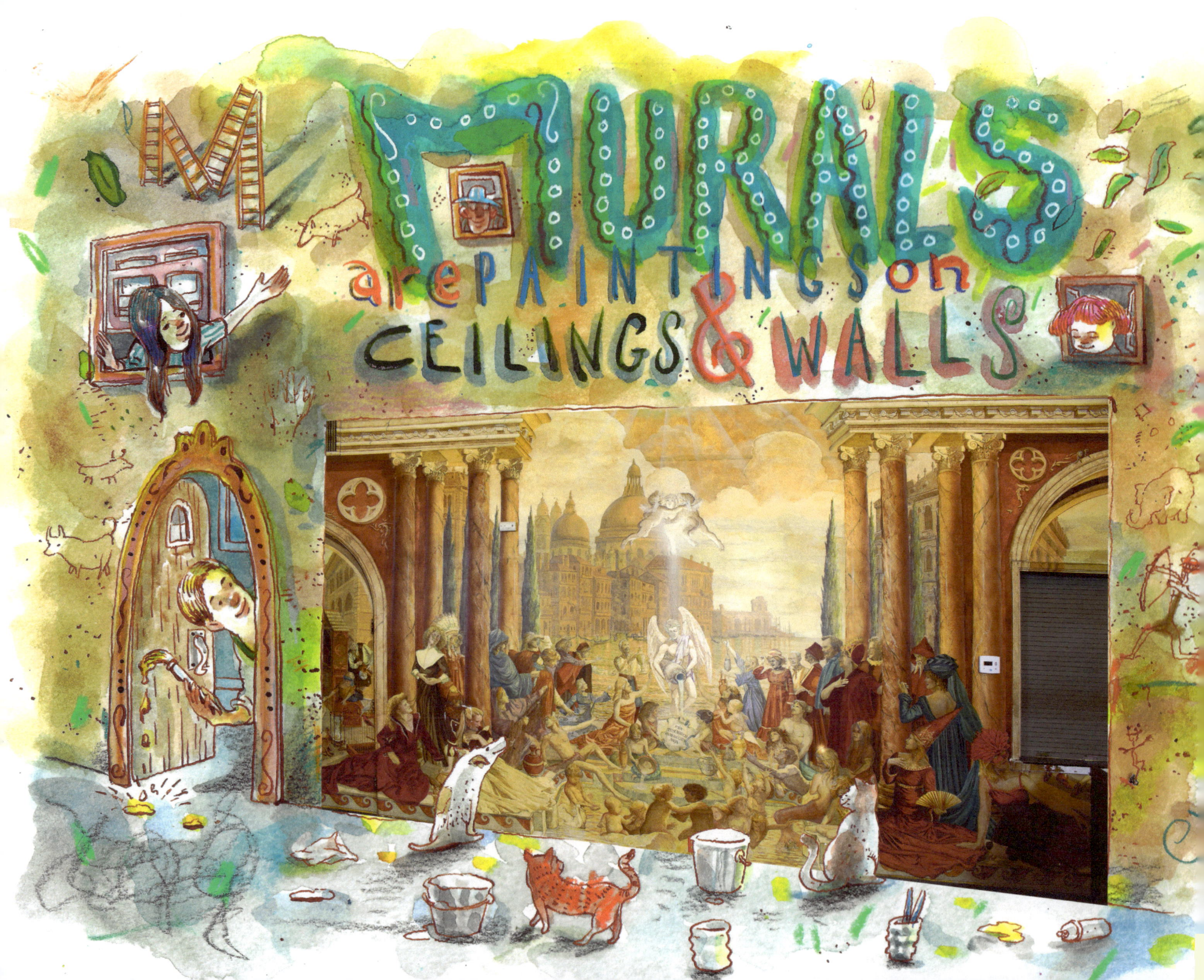

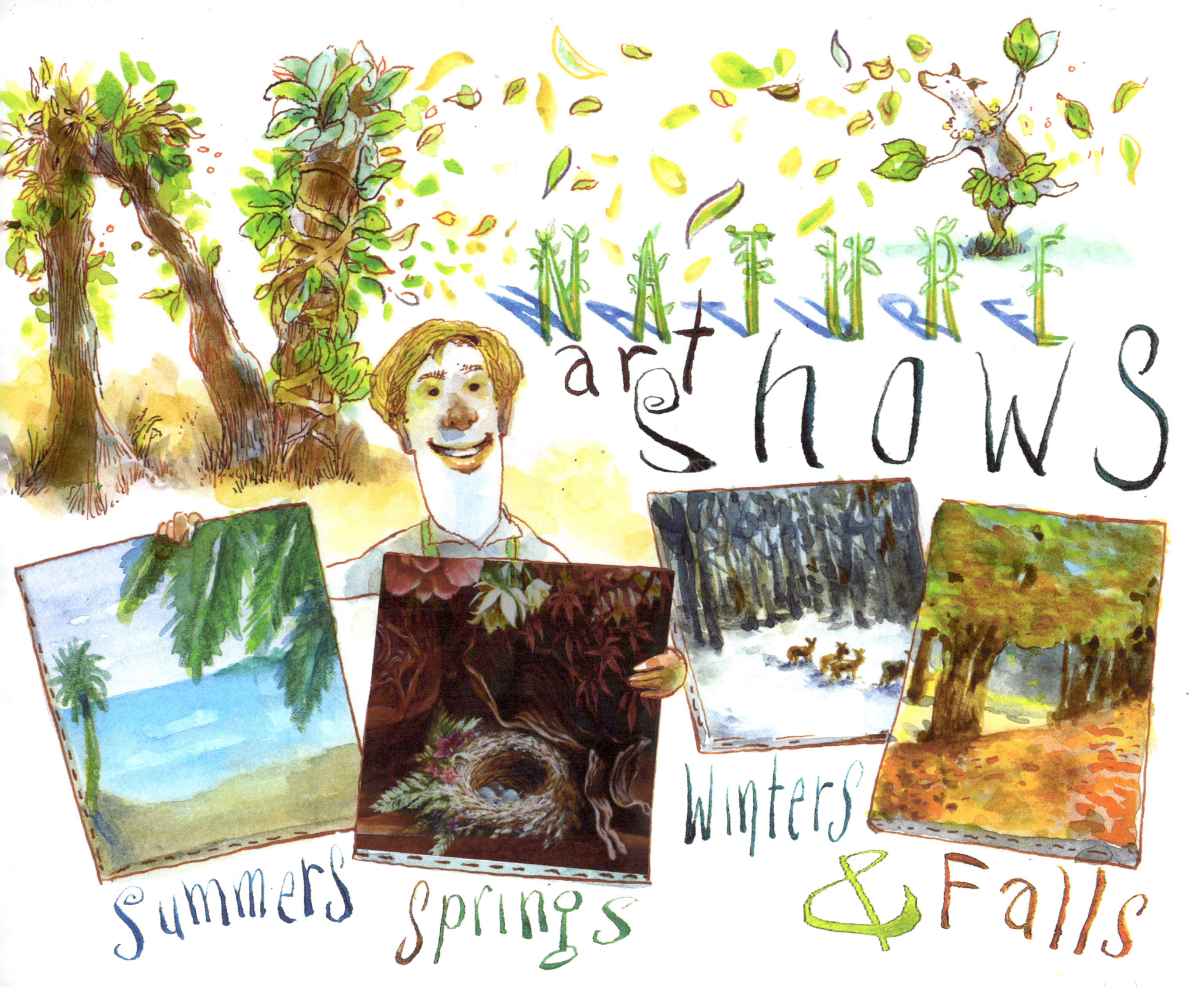

NATURE art shows

Summers Springs Winters & Falls

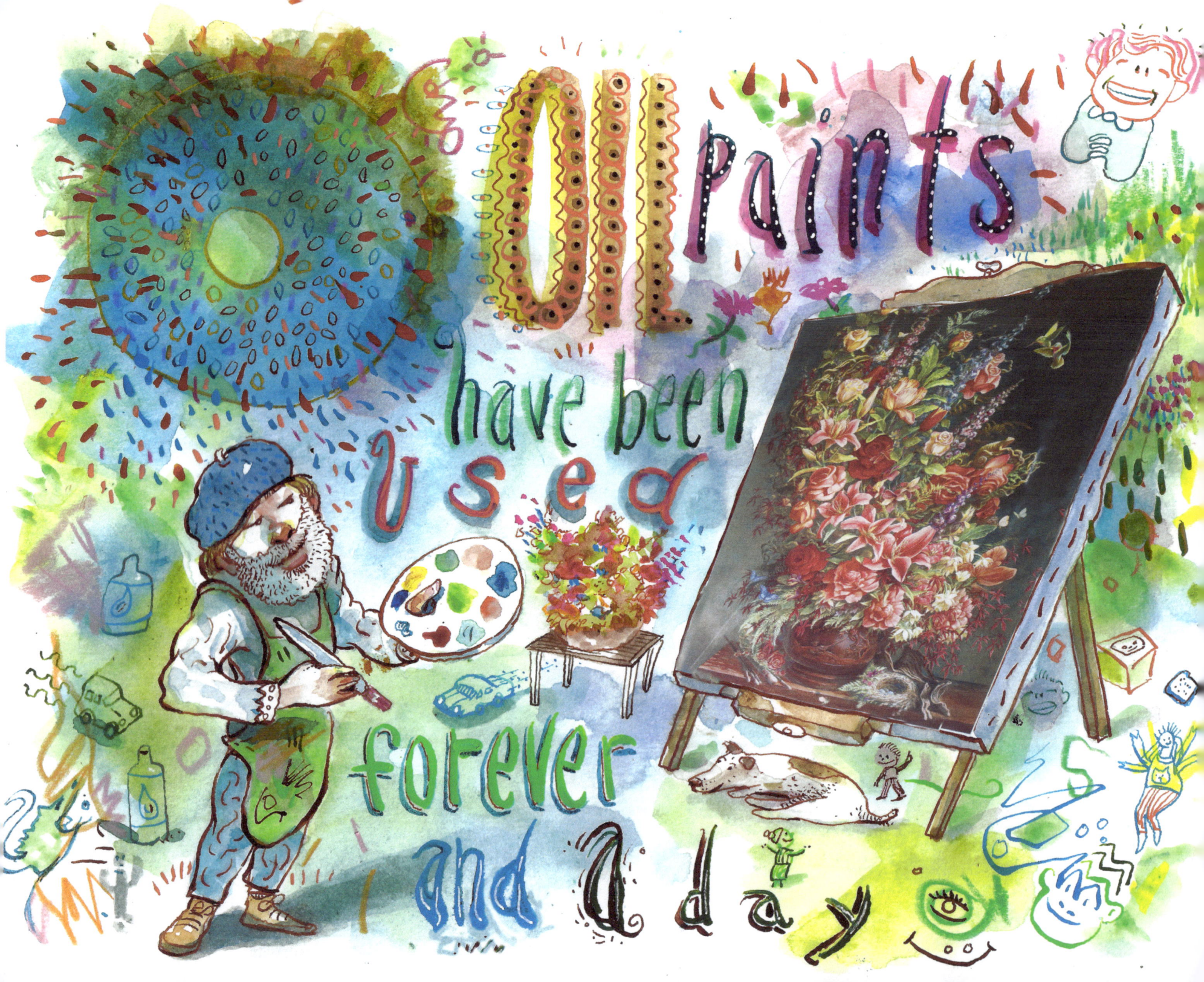

OIL paints have been used forever and a day

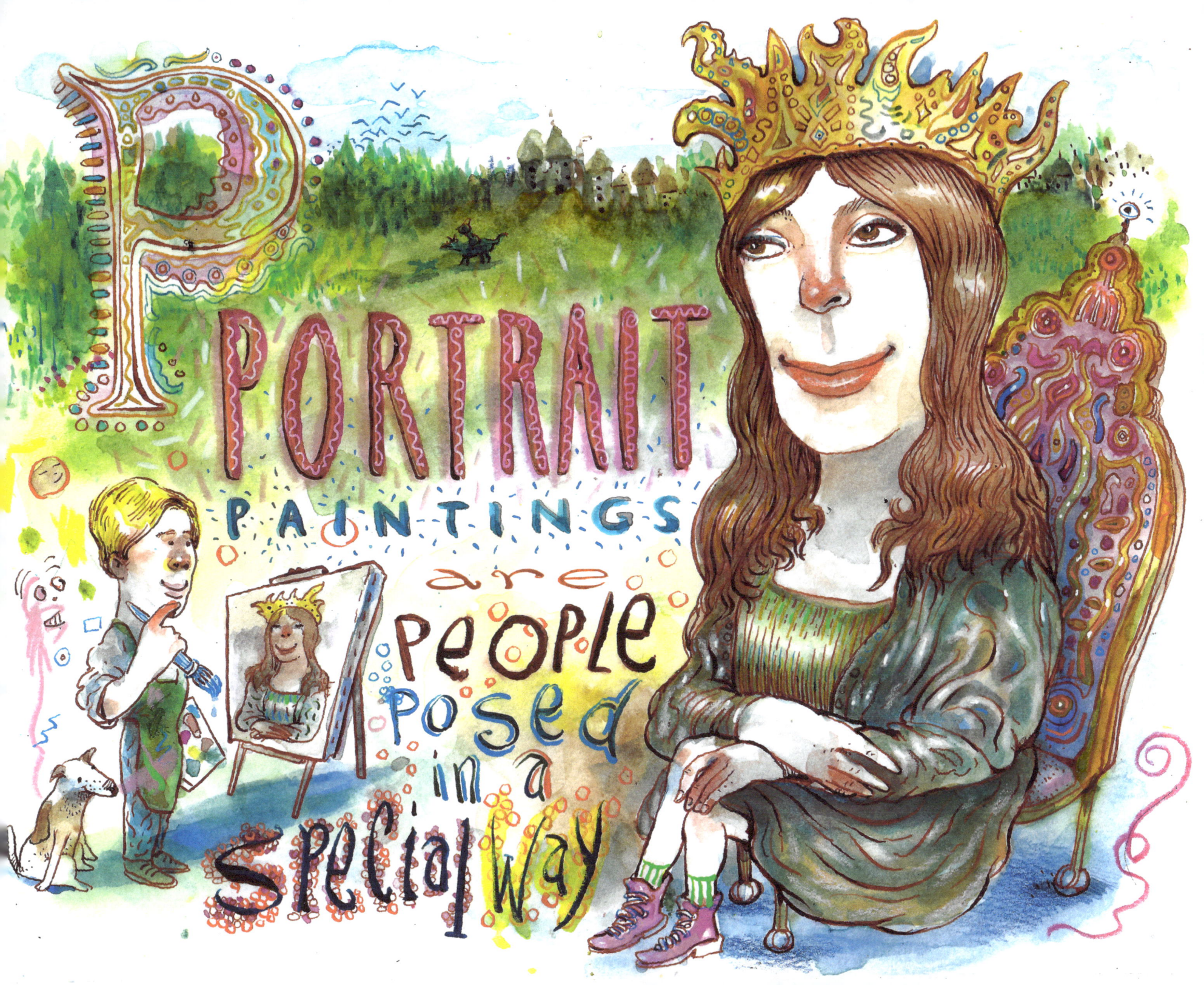

Portrait

PORTRAIT PAINTINGS are **people posed in a special way**

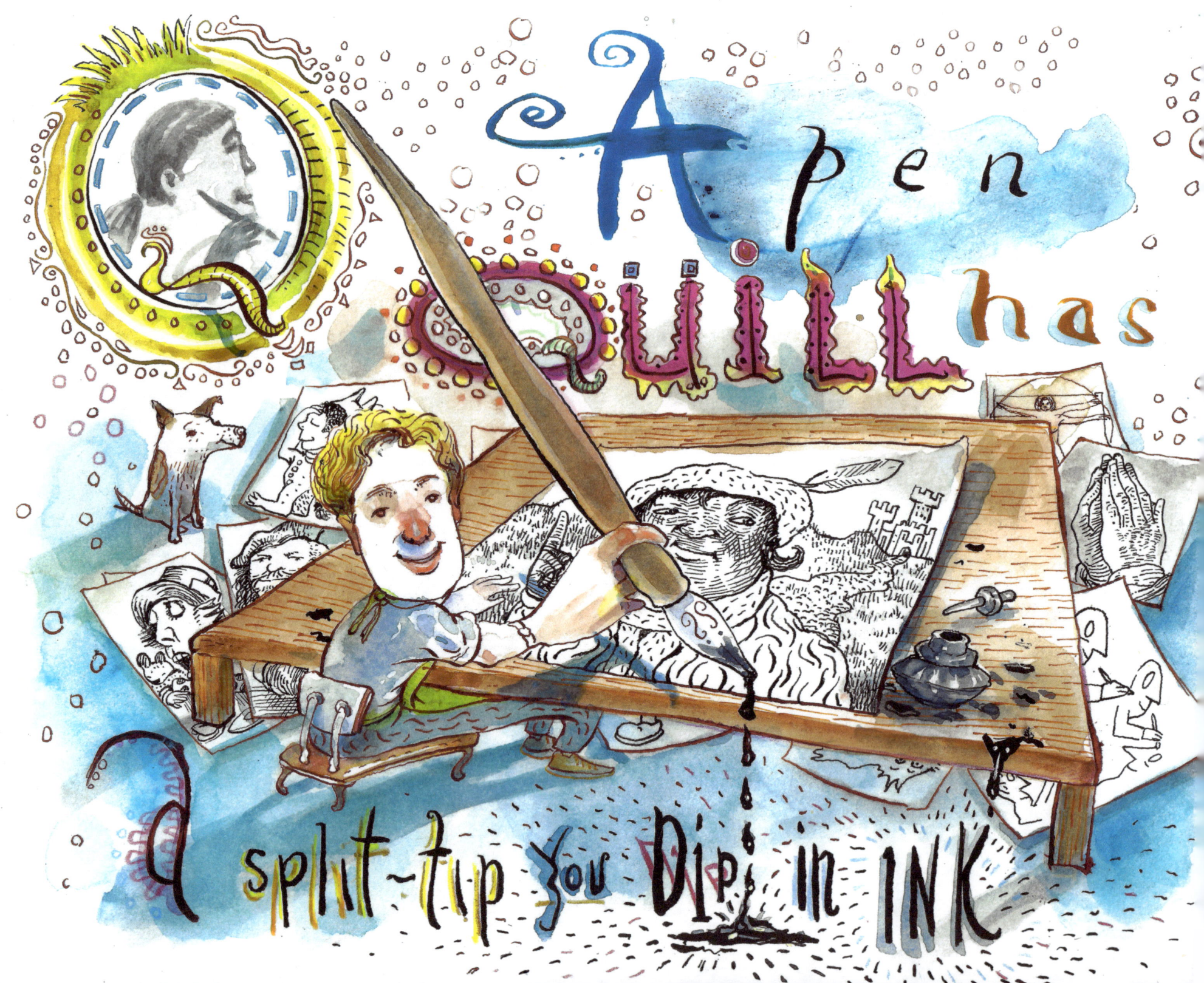

A pen QUILL has a split-tip you DiP in INK

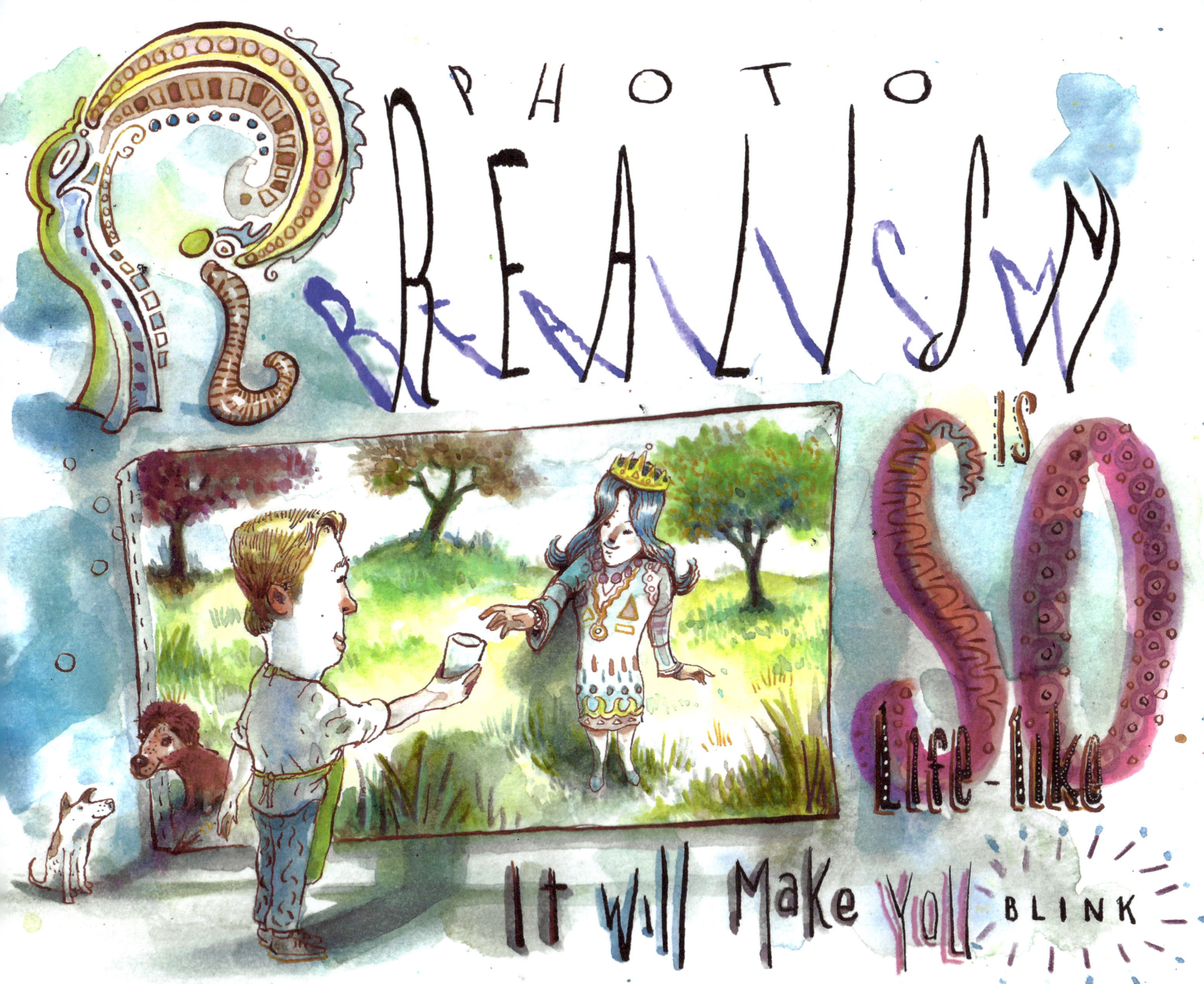

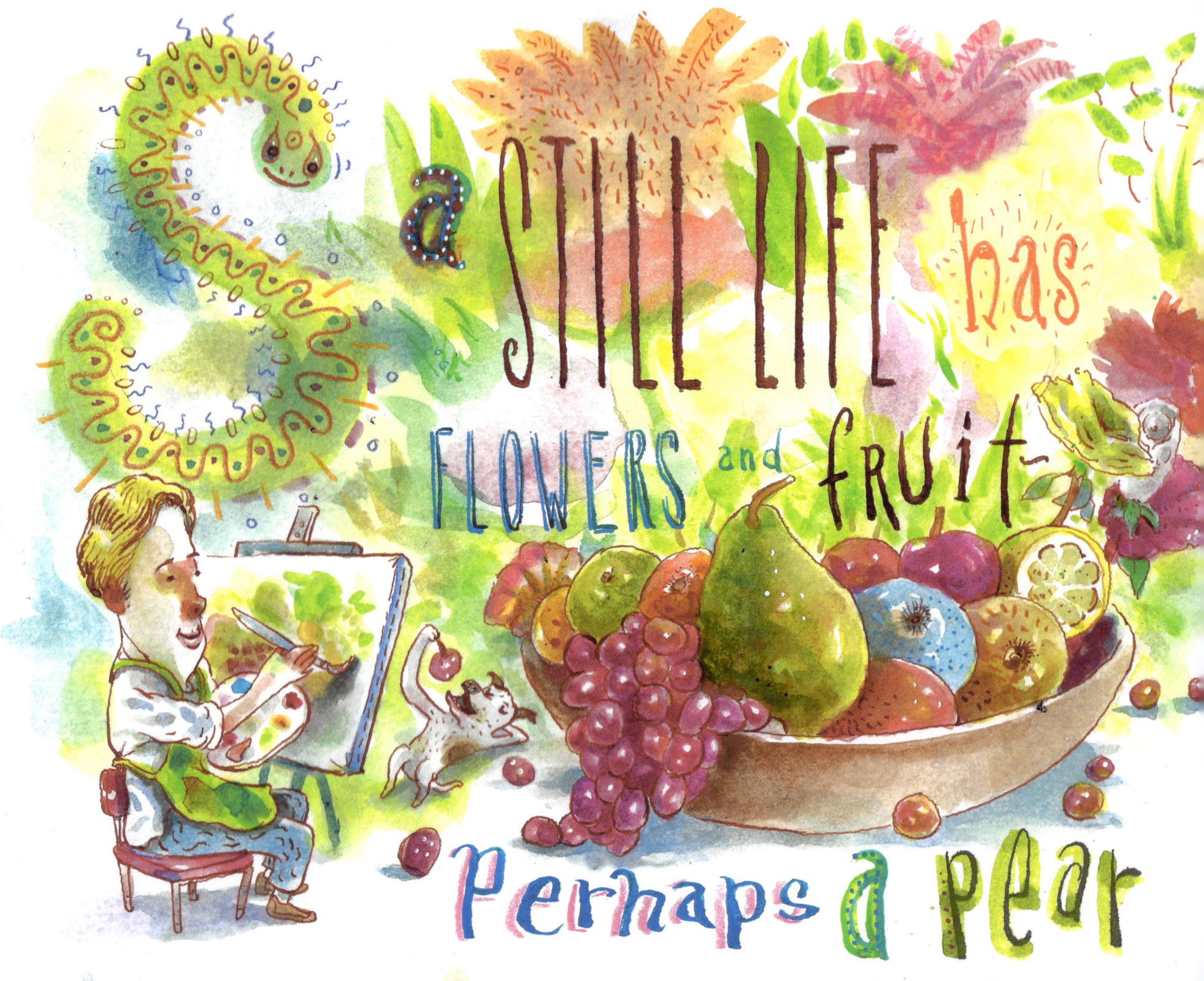

a STILL LIFE has FLOWERS and fruit-

perhaps a pear

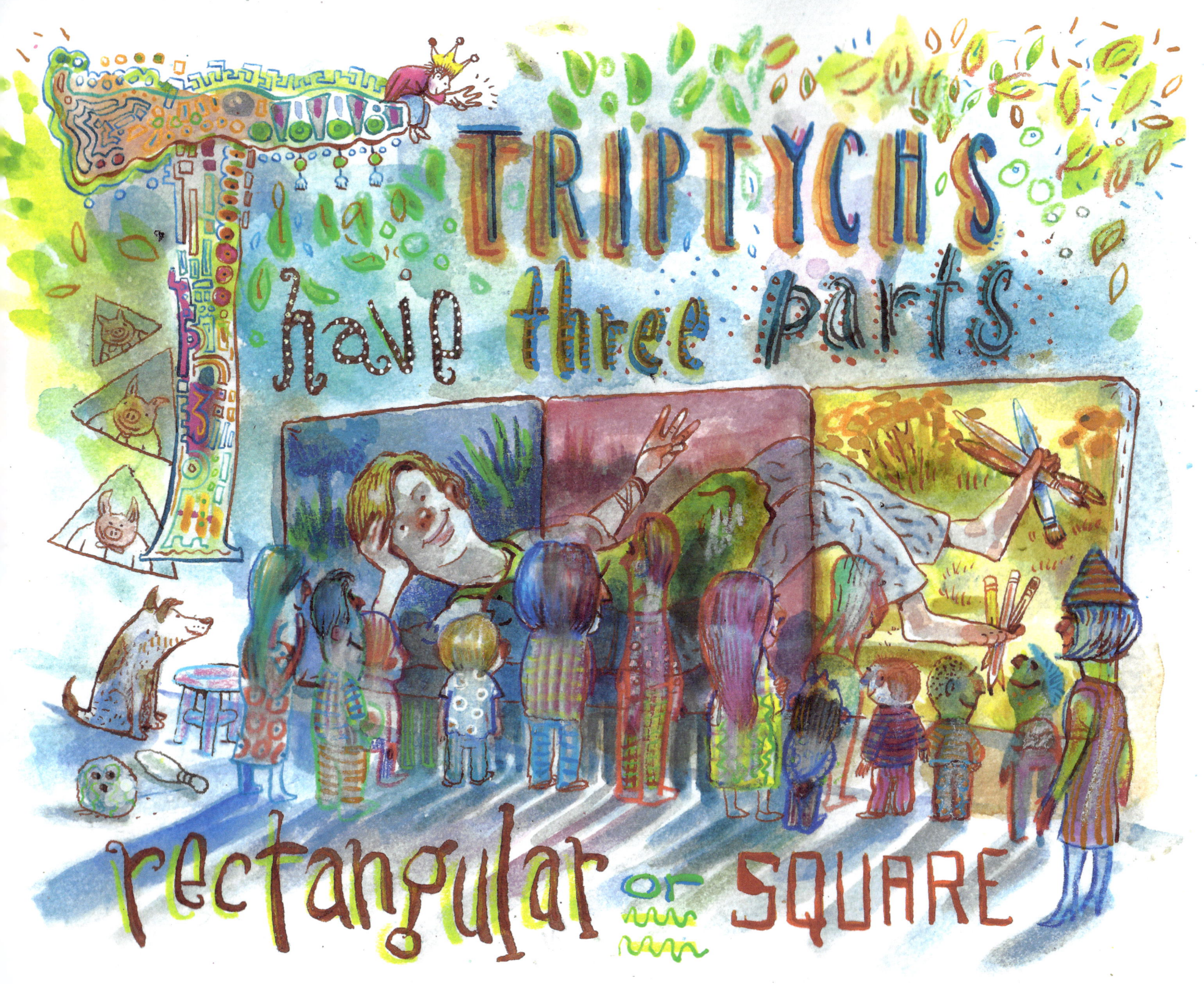

TRIPTYCHS have three parts

rectangular or SQUARE

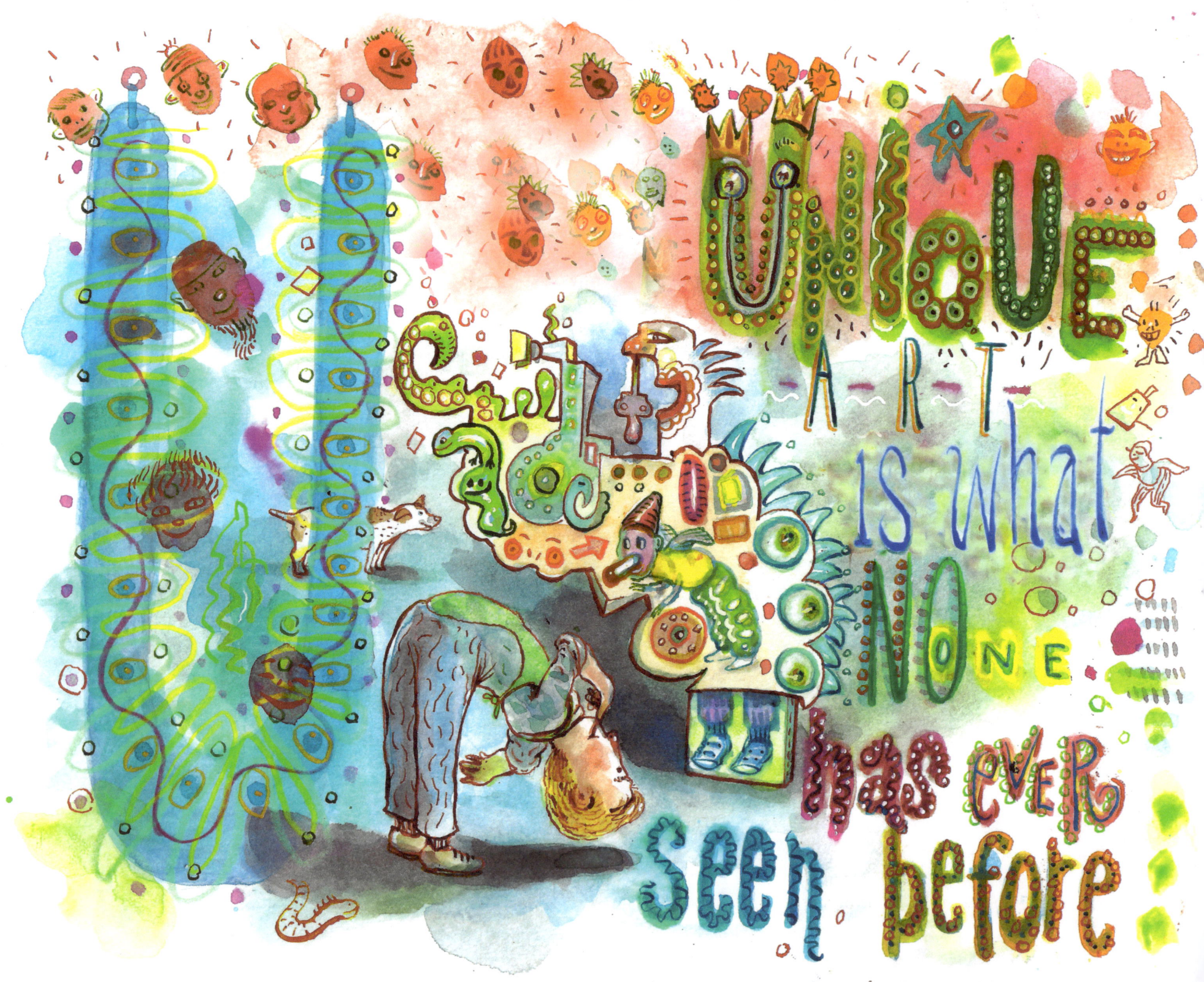

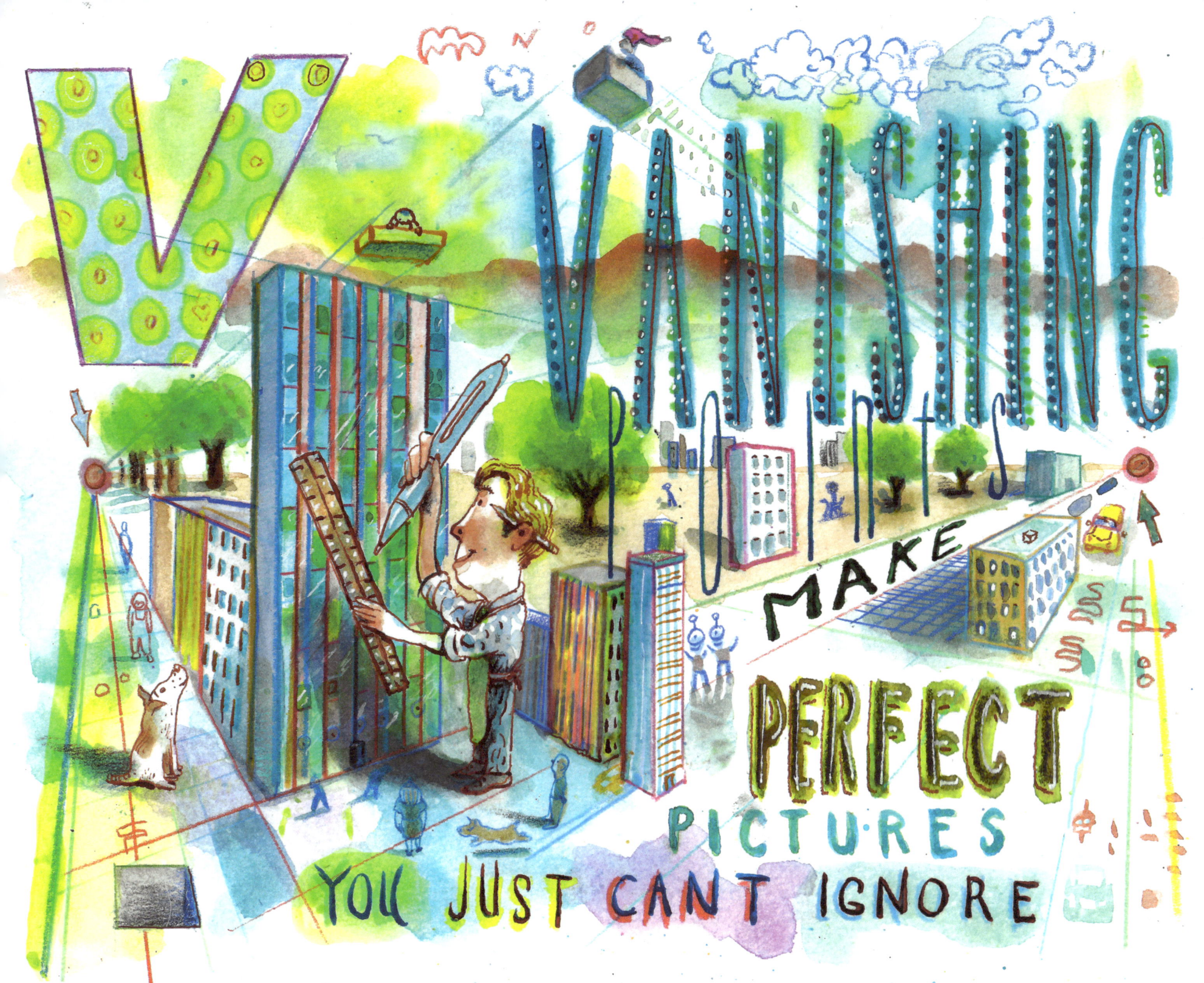

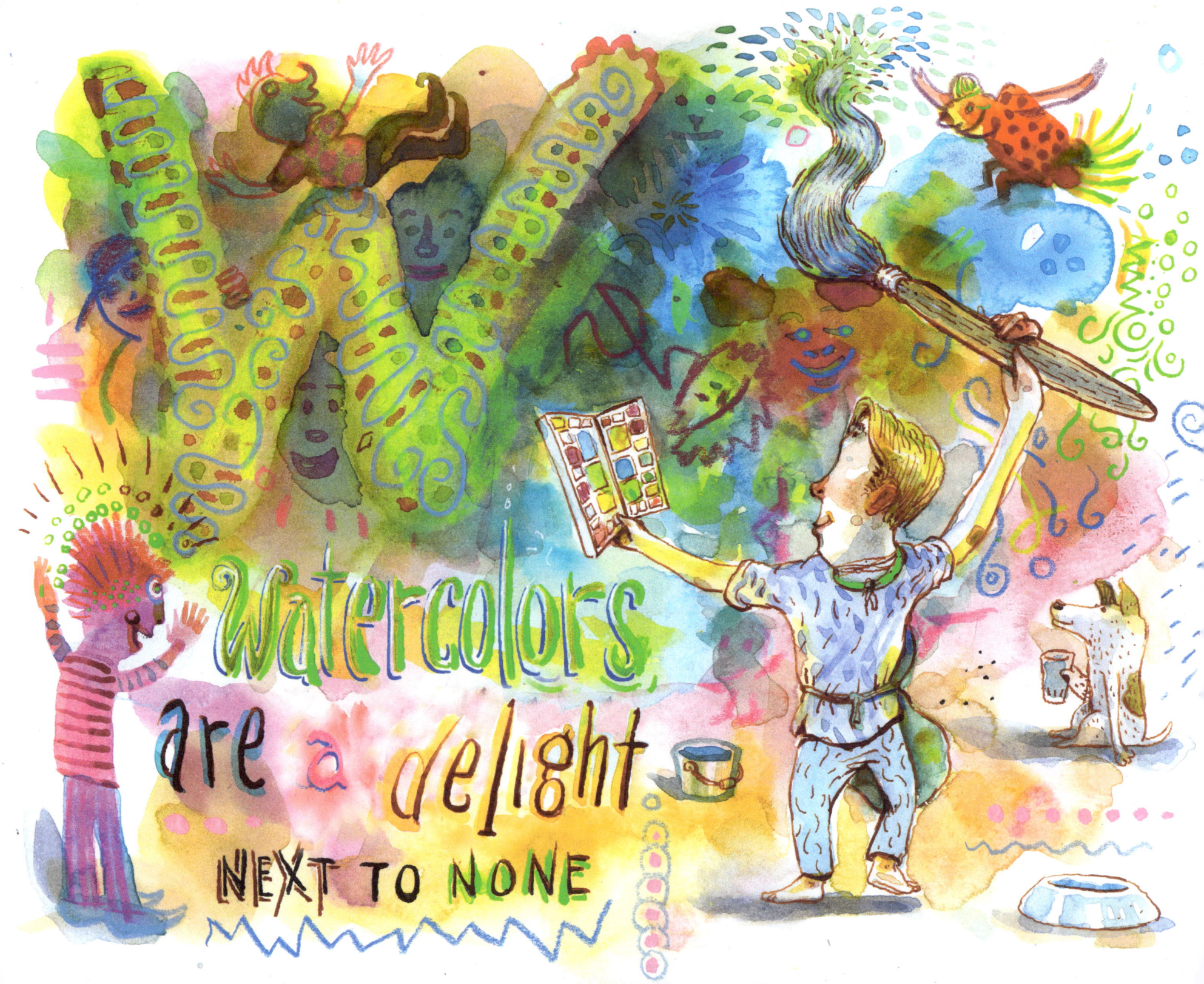

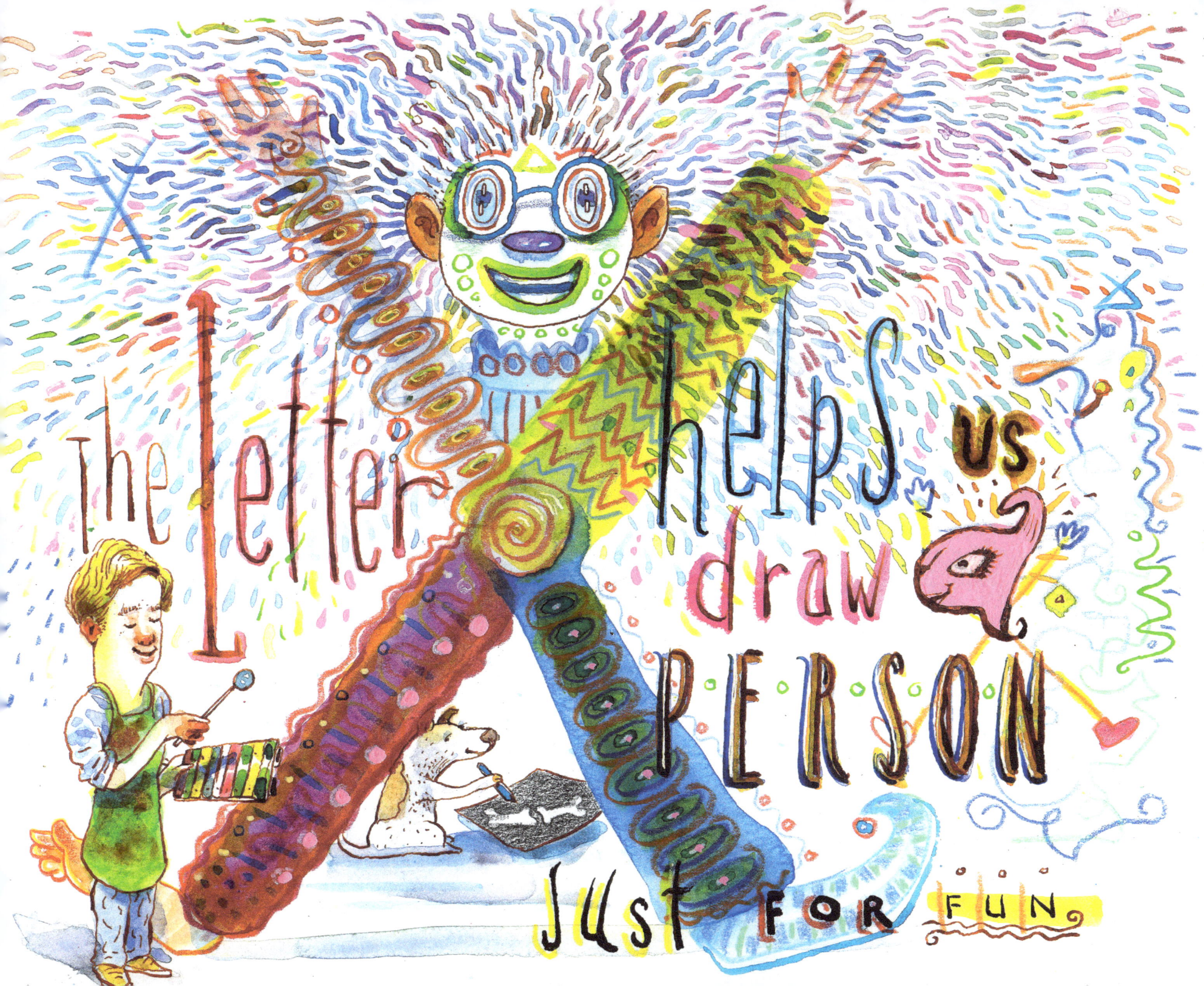

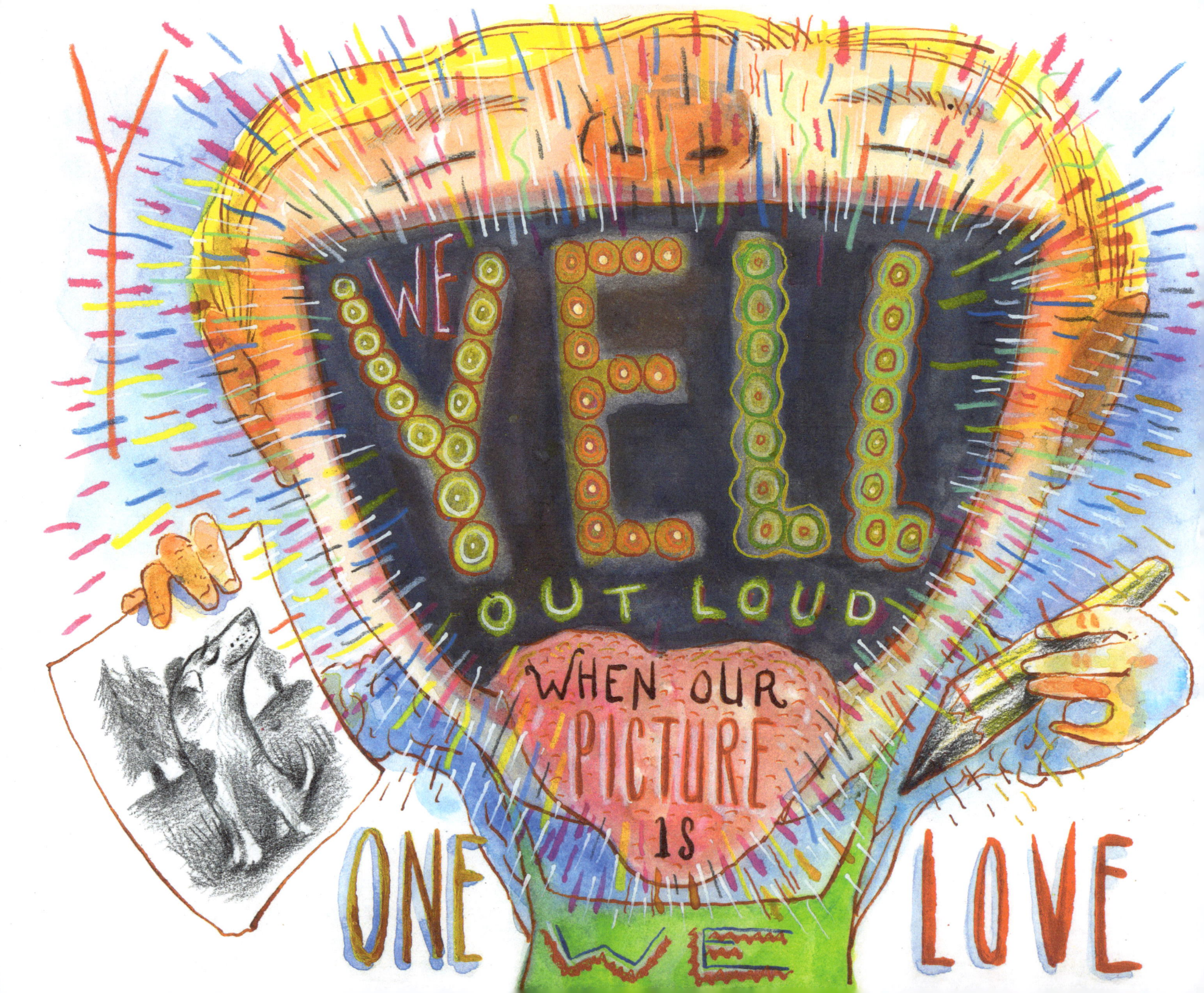

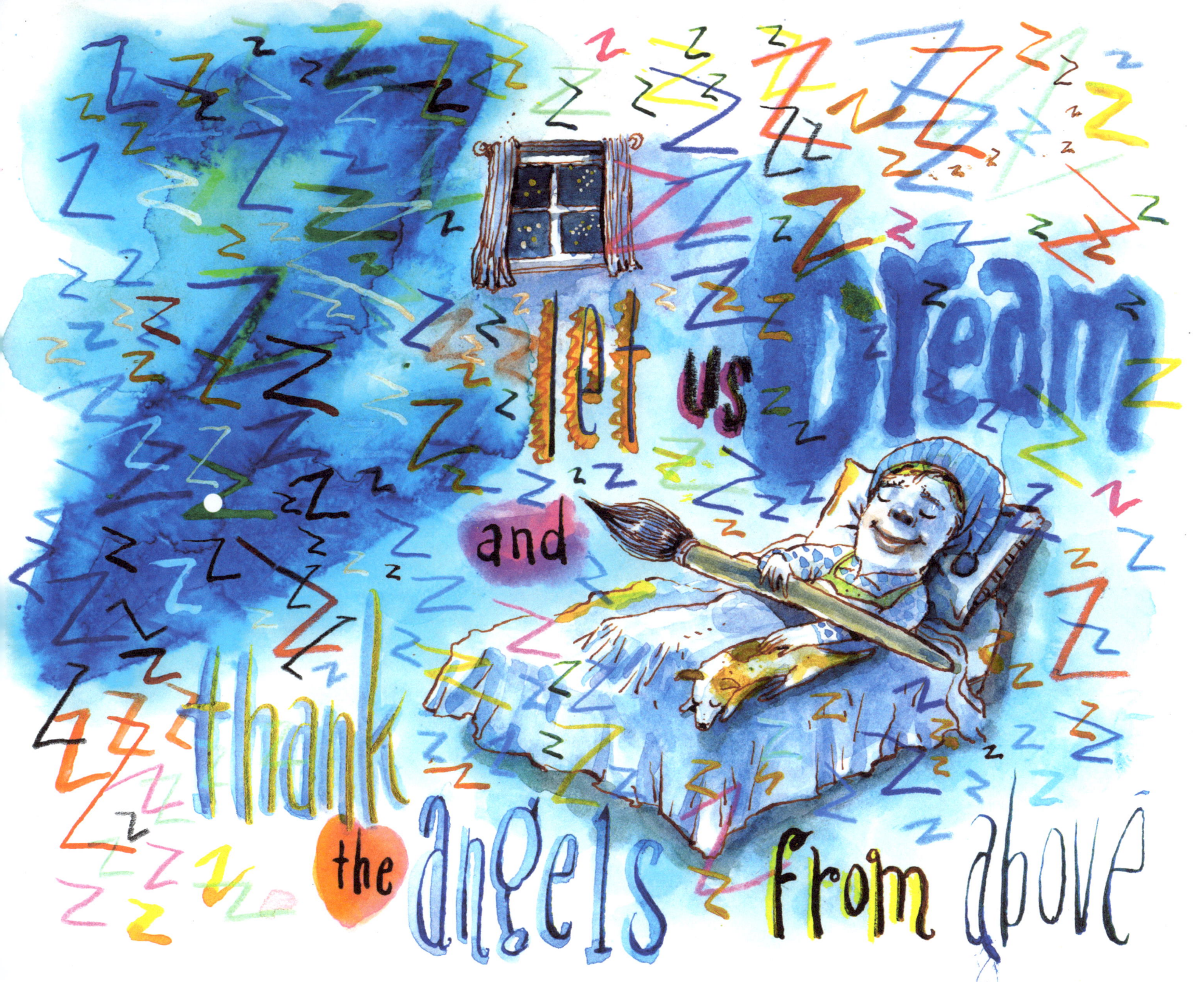

Now, let's make our own
masterpiece here.

A Guide to Russ & Iggy's Hidden Art Treasures

Sprinkled throughout the book are Russ and Iggy's homages to famous painters and sculptors.

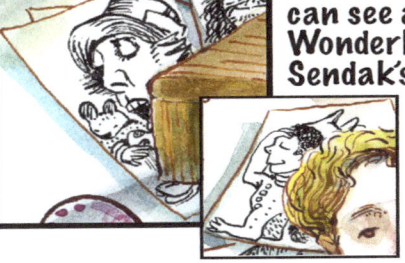

On the inside right front cover page, you can see Jeff Koons' famous Balloon Dog, which sold at auction in 2013 for more than 50 million dollars! Also on that page is an homage to Bill Watterson's Calvin and Hobbes, a comic strip that ran in newspapers from 1985 to 1995.

Russ is using a crayon on the Lithographs page to reference Honore Daumier, a French printmaker, caricaturist and painter who lived from 1808 to 1879.

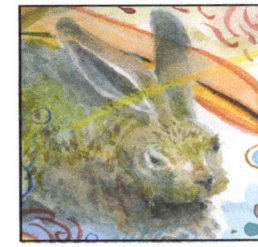

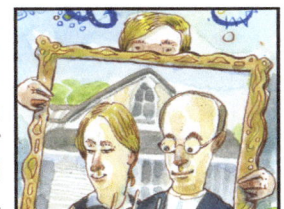

On the inside left back cover page, is a reference to Young Hare, a 1502 watercolor by German painter and printmaker Albrecht Dürer, who lived from 1471 to 1528.

On the Frames page, Russ is holding up his version of the 1930 painting, American Gothic, by Grant Wood, who lived from 1891 to 1942.

Russ is drawing with a pen quill on the Quills page, where you can see an illustration of The Mad Hatter from Alice In Wonderland by John Tenniel. There is also a nod to Maurice Sendak's Max from Where the Wild Things Are.

Since the History page is all art ever, it's filled with lots of different works. David is a masterpiece of Renaissance sculpture created in marble between 1501 and 1504 by the Italian artist Michelangelo. You can also see The Scream, the popular name given to a painting created by Norwegian Expressionist artist Edvard Munch in 1893.

The Gallery page features a portrait of the 90-year old Japanese contemporary artist, Yayoi Kusama. There's also a nod to the French Neoclassicist, Jacques-Louis David and his painting, Napoleon Crossing the Alps.

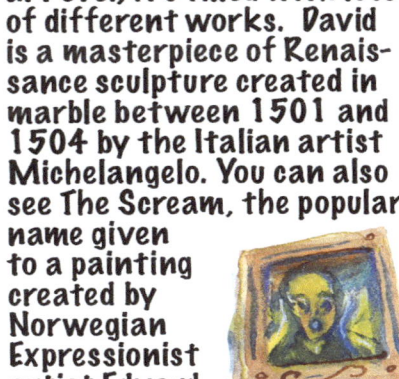

On the Impressionism page, Russ is working on a scene inspired by Claude Monet, one of the founders of French Impressionism. The 1899 painting Bridge at Giverny illustrates Monet's use of light to create dreamy imagery. Within Russ's painting are references to Vincent van Gogh and Georges Seurat. Iggy with an umbrella is a nod to Seurat's A Sunday Afternoon on the Island of La Grande Jatte.

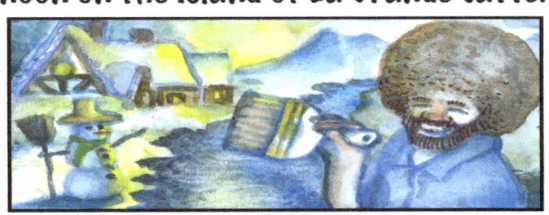

Kitsch art can make us laugh, and on this page, Russ is holding a painting that features a portrait of Bob Ross (host of the TV show, The Joy of Painting, which aired from 1983 to 1994 on PBS). Bob is shown in a painting that resembles the art of Thomas Kinkade, who referred to himself as Thomas Kinkade, Painter of Light. And just for fun, Iggy is wearing an Elvis wig.

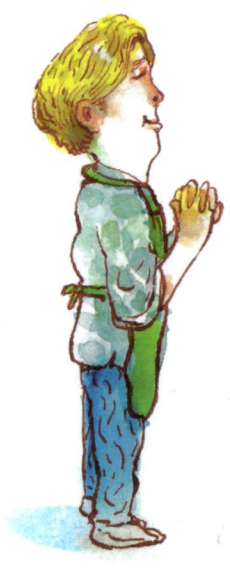

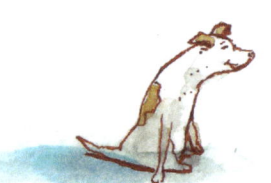

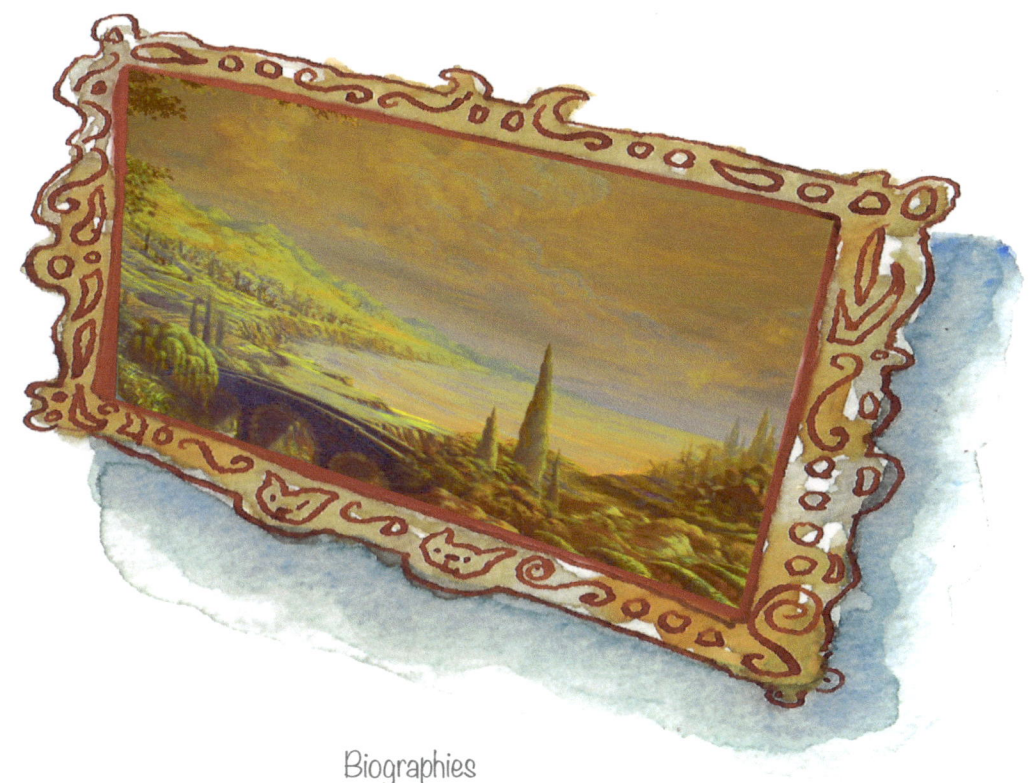

Biographies

Victoria Looseleaf

has loved words since she was a young girl growing up in Cleveland, Ohio. Since moving to Los Angeles,
her career as an author and award-winning arts journalist has taken her all over the world,
where she has interviewed thousands of fascinating people.
Victoria is passionate about art, life and kids of all ages.

JT Steiny

is an award-winning illustrator, painter, cartoonist and book designer.

Clinton Russell Butler

was an educator, artist and designer whose work can be seen in many institutions, including UC Irvine Medical Center
and the American Cancer Society, as well as at Temple Beth El of South Orange County, CA.,
and the Mizell Senior Center in Palm Springs. Butler, who also had numerous solo exhibitions,
passed away in 2017 of pancreatic cancer. He was a beloved figure who believed in arts education for all
children, and this book, the first in the *Russ & Iggy* Alphabet series, is his legacy.

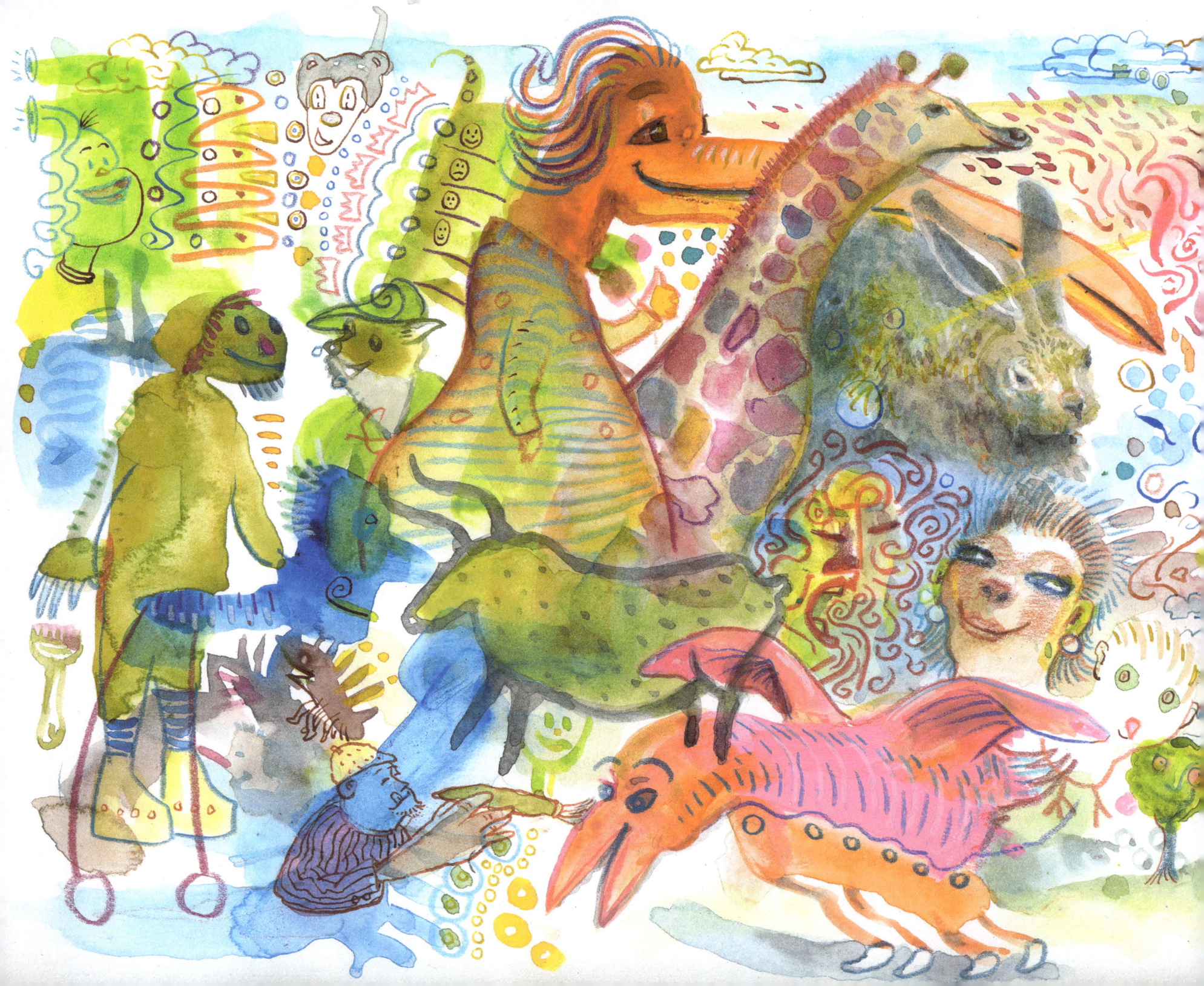